PREFACE

This guide represents the culmination of a dozen years of implementing large-scale changes, in many locales, with large and small, corporate and public organizations by Changeworks, our San Francisco consulting firm.

We are now sharing our knowledge with a wider audience. Our motivation is clear. While we feel that we may have some unique ways of packaging, framing and integrating these models and tools, they present the fruits of the experience of thousands of organizational change and transformation professionals, inside and outside organizations, and of the thirty years of research and development in the field.

The insights that formed the field of organizational development in the 1960s, when we entered it, remain critical to the success of this journey:

- People (employees, leaders) want opportunities to express their capability to learn and grow within the organization.

- People are more committed when they have input into decisions and share in planning change.

- People have untapped capacity and willingness to change, even though it may seem like they resist it at first.

- Leaders who let go of control, and do not try to manage every aspect of the process, will succeed more fully than those who do not.

However, in the recent push for quick and monumental change by increasingly desperate organizations, some of these lessons have been forgotten or ignored. In our work we have had the opportunity to work closely with change management groups of three of the largest consulting firms in the world. While they do many things quite well, each consulting firm feels that they have been less than effective at *mobilizing the human capacity to change.* As a result, many of their large change projects have been less successful than they would have liked.

This volume is meant to guide the initiators and leaders of change, both inside organizations and outside them, in designing and implementing change that really works. It is about initiating a process of change that involves people, using their capabilities and ultimately adds to the value of the organization by creating a capacity for continual change.

We present a methodology for the human side of change. The volume will not focus on any particular type of organizational redesign, such as moving to a process or customer focus, how to craft a new vision or changing strategic direction. Rather, we feel that each of these types of change needs to be based upon the foundation of collaborative involvement that we present here. The particular change initiative can then be implemented using the key activities of this framework.

We focus particularly on how to mobilize participation through all levels of the organization and to build commitment and capability for sustained change. We find that when people do not take into consideration how complex and difficult it is to change people and organizations, they tend to implement incomplete, imperfect or poorly thought-through efforts. The major challenge facing organizations, especially as we go into the new century, is how to get people and organizations to change in the directions that are abundantly clear to all of us.

GETTING YOUR ORGANIZATION TO CHANGE

A Guide For Putting Your Strategy Into Action

by
Dennis T. Jaffe, Ph.D. and Cynthia D. Scott, Ph.D., M.P.H.

Illustrated by Janet Schatzman

Crisp Publications
Menlo Park, CA

GETTING YOUR ORGANIZATION TO CHANGE

A Guide For Putting Your Strategy Into Action

Dennis T. Jaffe, Ph.D. and Cynthia D. Scott, Ph.D., M.P.H.

Credits
Managing Editor: *Kathleen Barcos*
Editor: *Andrea Reider*
Cover Design: *Fifth Street Design*
Typesetting: *ExecuStaff*

Copyright 1999 by Changeworks, Inc.

Printed in the United States of America by Bawden Printing
http://www.crisp-pub.com

Distribution to the U.S. Trade:

National Book Network, Inc.
4720 Boston Way
Lanham, MD 20706
1-800-462-6420

99 00 01 02   10 9 8 7 6 5 4 3 2 1

Library of Congress Catalog Card Number 98-072275
Jaffe, Dennis and Cynthia Scott
Getting Your Organization to Change
ISBN 1-56052-483-9

CONTENTS

PREFACE iii

ACKNOWLEDGEMENT vi

GETTING READY 1
    Overview—Building the Context for Change 1
    Setting the Course 3
    Steering the Effort—The Change Navigator 7
    Sustaining the Course—It's the People 16
    Initiating a Change—Getting Started 22

WAVE ONE: Mobilizing the Organization for Change **31**
    Wave One: Introduction **33**
    Task 1: Align Top Leadership **37**
    Taks 2: Convene and Charter the Change Team **47**
    Taks 3: Develop Individual Change Capability **59**
    Task 4: Assess Organizational Change Capability **81**

WAVE TWO: Designing the New Organization **113**
    Wave Two: Introduction **115**
    Task 1: Make the Case for Change **117**
    Task 2: Design New Work Processes and Culture **131**
    Task 3: Initiate Employee Involvement Processes **145**
    Task 4: Align Systems with New Processes **161**

WAVE THREE: Sustaining the Transformation **175**
    Wave Three: Introduction **177**
    Task 1: Champion New Ways **179**
    Task 2: Cascade Change Leadership **189**
    Task 3: Develop New Teams **223**
    Task 4: Anchor Organizational Learning **233**

ORGANIZATIONAL CHANGE WAVE-MAP **251**

ACKNOWLEDGEMENTS

Many colleagues have shared their learning on our journey. We first want to thank the other current and former members of Changeworks—especially Michael Stark, Glenn Tobe, Nancy Raulston, Mary Diggins, Nooshin Navidi and Elizabeth Demaray, out of many. Kathryn Goldman helped us with early drafts of the leadership sections. We want to thank our many consulting partners in the large consulting firms, our clients and our network of partner consultants we work with on change projects. We also thank Saybrook Graduate School, a mid-career, distance learning graduate school, which offered Dennis Jaffe a place to develop new ideas and the opportunity to meet the creative and exciting practitioners around the world who are its students and faculty.

GETTING READY

OVERVIEW—BUILDING THE CONTEXT FOR CHANGE

As an organization plans a major change, the key element in long-term success is the ability of the workforce to change quickly and accurately amid many uncertainties.

Most large-scale organizational change efforts have not achieved their objectives. They were either aborted before implementation, went awry as they began, or never developed the expected business results for the organization. While the successes were few, those who succeeded at change experienced a huge competitive advantage over companies that were unable to change.

Change fails because people see change through eyes that are accustomed to business as usual, rather than those of people who know how to be leaders of change. Change is a human and technical skill, that is naturally present in only a small number of executives. The others have to develop their skills in creating change.

Getting people to understand, become involved with and committed to change is the key task of organizations today. Leaders have to become leaders of change. Instead of blaming their people for not changing, leaders need to see that the success of change depends on their ability to understand its nature and lead people through it.

What Is Organizational Change?

The word change is used so much by organizations that its meaning has been diminished. Minor shifts in procedures and technology, and small differences in the external environment have been labeled as "changes." People all agree that change is happening everyday, but they are less clear about what they are expected to do about the changes. Anything new and novel that appears on the horizon is labeled change!

The word "change" refers both to a shift which occurs in the organization's external environment as well as the response to that shift on the inside of the organization (i.e., dealing with the changes that the organization makes to respond to external shifts, or in anticipation of external shifts). For purposes of clarification the term *environmental change* will be used to refer to external shifts and the word *change* will refer to the organization's response.

> ENVIRONMENTAL CHANGE = EXTERNAL SHIFTS

> CHANGE = ORGANIZATION'S RESPONSE

Another issue is the degree of change. Both "little c" and "Big C" changes are taking place. These are sometimes referred to as incremental and breakthrough (or revolutionary) change. The difference lies in the depth of the change. Many organizations today are proposing "Big C" changes that affect all parts and layers of the organization. The organization that is changing must look at change as taking place at multiple levels and groups. The process must be coordinated and integrated.

Saying "yes" to change means very little unless the organization sets up an infrastructure to accomplish it. The key tasks of the infrastructure to support change include:

- A persuasive story of why change is necessary
- A shared vision of where the organization is going
- Total involvement of every part of the organization
- Gatherings of all people involved to be informed and design together
- Continual two-way communication to everyone
- Clear, fairly implemented policies for workforce transition
- Investment in the resources to support the transition
- Training in new roles and skills
- Support for people's personal difficulty with change
- Transition structures to manage design and implementation
- Challenging people to question old ways and consider new paths
- Learning of new ways by individuals and the organization
- Personal support for the stress of change

SETTING THE COURSE

Commonly used change models may utilize three, four or even five phases, but all of the phase models make roughly the same point:

> *Change proceeds in waves that begin with waking up to the need to change and unhooking from the old ways, through a period of discovery and design of a new organization, and finally, into a period of implementing the new path with each person which affects the very core of the organization.*

Our three-phase model comes from the pioneering work of Kurt Lewin, and has been more recently adopted by Noel Tichy and other change theorists. While the three phases are not distinct sets of events (i.e., they tend to flow into one another and move at different speeds through different parts of the organization), it is relatively easy to determine if the organization is 1) getting ready to change, 2) designing the change, or 3) putting change into action.

Waves or Phases of Change

In order to divide the implementation of change into its three major phases and give a mental picture of their flowing nature, each phase has been called a WAVE.

WAVE ONE: *Mobilizing the Organization for Change*
This frequently neglected phase is where the organization gets a wake-up call and everyone is put on alert to get with the process. The whole organization learns the story of why they have to change and the reason for the changes that are being set in motion. Rather than keep change a secret in the early phases, the whole organization must be engaged in the process.

WAVE TWO: *Designing the New Organization*
Every part of the organization takes a role in the creation of a map for proposed change. People seek new models, exchange information and envision the future organization. This is exciting and demanding work.

WAVE THREE: *Sustaining the Transformation*
The organization puts the change into action with a vast and difficult learning process which impacts every person. To the degree that people have been prepared and part of the prior process, they are ready to take up the challenge.

The other element concerns the four LEVELS of the organization that are involved in creating change. Each level has a different perspective or place in successful change.

FIRST LEVEL: *Top Leadership*
This level consists of the *Executive Team* of the organization (or business unit) under whose umbrella the change occurs, who provide the necessary resources and visibly and actively support the change. It contains the *Change Sponsor,* the person who makes the decision to carry out the change. This person must be active, not in controlling the process, but in inspiring people to take part in the change.

SECOND LEVEL: *The Change Team*
This level includes the *Change Leader* and the *Change Navigator.* The Change Leader is the operational leader of the team or group that must change. This person leads the change team and the group that implements the change. Many people may be the change leaders, but there should be one person who takes the responsibility for the change. Once a person shifts from being a manager to being a change leader, he or she must adapt a different perspective and use new skills. The Change Leader is also part of the Top Leadership Team. The Change Leader delegates activities to the other members of the Change Team and the Change Navigator.

The Change Navigator is a partner with the Change Leader and designs the process for creating change and acts as the guide for the Change Team. Change Navigators may be either internal or external consultants. They may also be line managers, or members of human resources, information systems, or support functions.

Change Navigator—guides the process
Change Leader—responsible for the outcome

THIRD LEVEL: ***Employee Involvement***
This level includes the people that are affected by the change—those who have to do the changing. They are represented in the change process through the *Employee (or Stakeholder) Involvement* activities through which the organization as a whole will become aware of, involved in and committed to the change.

Stakeholders are those who are affected by the change. These people may be in the organization itself, or they may be outside the organization, like customers, suppliers and spouses of the employees. All stakeholders need to be involved frequently and early in the process.

This level contains those that are directly under the authority of the Change Leader; these are the *Team Members.* They must make the most difficult changes and need to develop a real commitment to learning new skills and ways of working together.

FOURTH LEVEL: ***Organizational Culture and Process***
This level refers to the deep structure of the organization where the values, structures, policies and core processes are stored. It is often called the *Organizational Culture.*

If this level is not aligned with the desired changes, change will not "take," and it will not last. This level is beyond the people and represents the foundation of the organization.

The chart on the following page will show you how the waves and levels interact with each other in order to create change. Each wave contains four key tasks that take place at each level of change.

FRAMEWORK FOR DESIGNING CHANGE

	Wave One Mobilize	**Wave Two** Design	**Wave Three** Transform
Level One TOP LEADERSHIP *Sponsor Executive Team*	Align Top Leadership	Make the case for change	Champion New Ways
Level Two CHANGE TEAM *Change Leader* *Change Navigator*	Convene and Charter Change Team	Design New Processes	Cascade Change Leadership
Level Three EMPLOYEE INVOLVEMENT *Team Members Stakeholders*	Develop Individual Change Capabilities	Employee Involvement Process	Develop New Teams
Level Four ORGANIZATIONAL CULTURE AND PROCESSES	Asses Organizational Change Capabilities	Align Systems With New Processes	Develop New Teams

In the chapters that follow, there are key tasks for each wave of each level, activities, expected outcomes, challenges, and guiding principles with a description of the activities of each task. The tasks also contain specific Change Navigational Tools, which are templates for specific interventions, workshops, or processes which are key to that element of change.

STEERING THE EFFORT—THE CHANGE NAVIGATOR

A Change Navigator is a person who guides the process of change, but who has not the direct power to implement changes or programs. He or she is the guide and coach for the Change Team, and other Change Leaders. The Navigator has influence without authority or direct line responsibility. The Navigator is recruited by the Change Leader or Sponsor to help steward change through the organization. It is too difficult and demanding a role for the Change Leader to take on.

Change Navigators teach and help develop new skills, and offer a broad, multi-organizational experience of overcoming change-related challenges. They sometimes challenge the organization to do what it takes to implement change, even if they are internal employees.

Change Leaders get the ear of the people in the organization, develop commitment through the organization, and create plans that fit the culture of the organization. They must lead the process of change and develop the capability to lead the next round of change.

Change Navigation is an example of an approach to organizational change that is known as **Process Consulting**. Its goal is to develop organizational capability inside the organization, rather than providing expert solutions that tell people what to do. In doing that, the Navigator becomes a teacher as well as an expert, a coach as well as a player. To achieve capability transfer, the Change Navigator must work with the organization in a spirit of deep partnership and learning.

Change begins when a visionary organizational leader tries to create change. Behind the leader are many people, with different agendas and perspectives. Some will support the change while others will oppose it. The Change Navigator brings these disparate elements into alignment around the change.

The Navigator thus works through relationships with various elements of the organization, by designing learning processes and systems that help the people engaged in change to recognize, understand, and act upon the events that take place inside and outside the organization. This enables it to design, implement and sustain the changes necessary for them to remain competitive.

The Change Navigator is responsible for the climate of change in the organization, helping leaders and employees make changes that:

- Produce the desired results

- Solve unexpected problems as they come up

- Develop the capability for initiating future changes

When problems or change targets are ambiguous or not clearly defined, the Change Navigator must be able to slip outside the context of the organization; to envision the outcome of the process. He or she must say difficult and unpopular things to the leaders of the organization and bring unpleasant realities to light.

The Navigator is not just a teacher, but also a learner. He or she continually finds opportunities to receive feedback on how the process is going. This willingness to take responsibility and listen is what the Navigator wants the people who change to be willing to do, and he or she can only do this if they are willing to model that behavior. The ability to learn continually, to question one's own assumptions and to question what one knows is essential to success as a Change Navigator.

Change Navigators must explore their own personal beliefs, attitudes, biases, blinders and limitations that affect their ability to be helpful. This includes looking at their own personal values, mission and vision as a Change Leader, and how those inner orientations affect their own motivation, capability and performance.

The Difficulties of Change Relationships

While the positive aspects of having a Change Navigator seem so obvious, relevant and helpful to the organization, in fact, leaders often resist, or avoid creating the collaborative partnerships that are needed. There are several reasons for this:

- Employees are upset, confused, or facing uncertainty. They may fear, distrust or resent anyone who comes in with a change agenda.

- Operational leaders are under pressure to get things done, and they fear that the various political and personal agendas, issues and time for building relationships and collaboration, will take up all their energy and make them unsuccessful.

- Some leaders may feel caught in the middle. They have been told to do one thing by the leadership, but they hear a different understanding or expectations from those lower in the organization.

There are several common difficulties in creating change relationships that inhibit the initiation of the change process:

Challenges	Implications for Action
Change is not a logical process. It involves emotional issues for people.	The Navigator must understand and manage the emotional phases of transition, helping individuals, teams and leaders build adaptibility to change.
The Navigator works through other people.	The Navigator has to develop the skills of partnership and collaboration.
Organizational systems are complex systems. Changing one part effects the whole.	The Navigator has to adopt a systems perspective on the nature of change in organizations.

Collaborative change partnerships are essential to effecting change.

COLLABORATIVE PARTNERSHIPS

Collaborative change partnerships are the vehicle to initiating effective change within an organization. While they want to change, their leaders carry models and ideas about change that stem from traditional ideas of leadership as command and control. These models can change only very limited types of behavior, and do not offer guidelines for the far-reaching changes that are needed. In order to succeed at change, the organization needs to create a new model of how change occurs. This model is the *Collaborative Partnership Model* of change.

The Change Navigator starts by helping the leaders of the organization move toward adopting this model. Its principles and practices may seem very simple, but in practice, they are difficult, demanding, and require learning in order to practice.

Processes that Change Leaders Will Implement

Change Leadership develops **Change Capability** within an organization through collaborative partnerships that combine a model of active engagement and participation across the whole organization with a framework of critical focus areas that organize learning and action at each phase of a change process.

The Change Leaders must implement several types of process within the organization. These will be mentioned repeatedly in various phases and tasks of change.

The core principles of collaborative partnership include:

1. **Integrative, Systems Perspective.** Every part of the change process is connected to every part of the organization. Because of this interconnection, the integration of Change Leadership activities is critical to success. The process model allows the consultation to build appropriate involvement, link activities across boundaries and move from design to implementation toward achieving the highest level of results.

2. **Two-Way Communication.** This is the most mentioned and least followed process in change. People usually think that communication is telling people what to do. But think about a change. People are unlikely to change very much if they don't understand why and they don't make input to the changes. Communication by definition needs to be two-way, and people need to have a forum for sharing their reactions, concerns and feelings about change.

3. **Participation.** Effective change builds partnership in every activity, within a team that includes many Change Leaders, Navigators and Resources. Partnership combines the expertise of the Change Navigator with the experience and accountability of the Change Leader and his or her team, to jointly define the problems, the pathways, the outcomes and to solve problems as they arise.

   This is another overused and underdone process. The people who conduct a process need to be consulted about changes to their work. While people admittedly may be somewhat tied to the way they do things and find it hard to change, creating change by having outside experts tell people how to do their work differently has a long history of not working. The plans and designs of the Change Team and Change Leaders need to be run by the people who will be affected by the change and their needs discussed and integrated when appropriate.

4. **Learning.** Learning is more than changing behavior. In organizations today, successful change demands employees not just learning new skills, but learning to adapt different mindsets and different roles in the organization. They learn by a much more involved and active process of participation than is needed if they are just changing their behavior. Many of the activities of Change Navigators, Change Leaders, and Change Teams involve setting up workshops and large- and small-group events that produce not only change, but also learning.

5. **Alignment.** Refers to the degree to which people understand, commit and act upon what they say, or the degree to which one system, group or activity is connected to other related ones. The process of change continually demands that people need to look at the alignment of their words and their deeds—between what they do and what they want others to do, and between the results and pathways to the results. Change often founders because of lack of alignment.

6. **Cascading.** A change has to reverberate from the top or the middle to become part of the behavior of every part of the organization. It often erodes as it moves down the organization. The people at the top take time to plan, to build commitment, and to learn—then they expect the people below them to just get with it. They forget what they went through and their own learning process. The process of change needs to be recreated for each level of the organization.

> **7. Boundary Spanning.** People in organizations tend to see their functional groups as having a reality and solidity that must be maintained. The boundary between one group and another tends to become a barrier. People do not work with people from other teams, and they limit their interaction. They tend to pass work and tasks across the boundary, not work together. Most efforts at change involve breaking down these barriers and boundaries to create processes that have more open and fluid interaction.

The Qualities of a Good Change Navigator

An effective Change Navigator needs to utilize five key skills:

1. Communication

The Change Navigator acts as a communicator with all elements of the organization, developing not just awareness, but acceptance of the task within the organization.

Communication is not just with individuals or leaders, but includes developing processes to communicate clearly with teams and throughout the whole organization. It is not enough to have the top team or the steering committee on board. The Change Navigator has to monitor and initiate an organization-wide process of exchange and informing about the need for the change, the process that has been elected, and what is expected of individuals.

The more communication and awareness about change, the more there will be commitment and participation in the process. The Change Navigator must set up internal information networks to enable people throughout the organization to understand and foster exchange about the change processes.

In individual conversations or in group presentations, the following cycle will unfold:

- Present information simply and clearly

- Listen to responses, including feelings, without judgment or interruption

- Share your understandings and responses

- Clarify and amplify common understandings

- Move toward shared agreement or next steps in conflict resolution

2. *Conflict Resolution*

Throughout the organization there will be many points where the Change Navigator and leaders/employees will come upon conflicts, differences, and issues of concern and difficulty.

There are many types and levels of conflict. Conflict is not bad; it is inevitable, and stems from both varying interests and needs, and misunderstandings or confusion about what is really happening. There can be conflict between different groups, between leaders, and between different stakeholders.

Conflict resolution skill involves surfacing the areas of disagreement and finding ways to move the issue forward without avoiding or denying differences that are real. If these issues are swept under the rug, avoided or dealt with indirectly, the repercussions can threaten the success of the venture. The Navigator must learn to be comfortable raising issues, talking about differences and openly facing conflict, or else the rest of the organization cannot learn to do this.

The Navigator must raise the issue in a way that is helpful to the client and that enables them to work on that issue. This can be very difficult, especially when the client does not really want to hear about it.

The Navigator must define the possible conflict in a way that creates trust and openness, and reduces threat, blame, and antagonism, so that the conflict can be addressed constructively. The Navigator must avoid getting caught in political webs by opening dealing with vested interests and politics which can threaten real change. The Navigator must be an effective organizational negotiator and politician.

Ways to raise a difficult issue:

"I notice you doing this, and it seems to go against your intention to . . ."

"I'm feeling some discomfort with this, but I feel that it is important that we talk about . . ."

"I have heard, or observed this, and I feel you need to address this issue . . ."

3. Coaching and Teaching

Personal development and learning is a cornerstone of Change Leadership. Unless the leaders of an organization become learners and develop themselves, they cannot lead other people to make extensive changes.

A Change Navigator is a teacher, working with key leaders to learn how to manage change. Organization leaders will routinely come to them with their problems and ask them to solve them.

While there are some times when a solution is called for, more often they will have to help the leader see that he or she has the tools or the potential to solve the problem for himself or herself. This means that instead of offering an expert solution, the Navigator helps the person come to their own solution. This is called coaching or learning.

4. Facilitation

At the most basic level, Change Navigation involves arranging a series of group meetings to involve people in the design and implementation of the change. To manage these activities, the Navigator must exercise group skills such as facilitation of meetings, building a climate of openness and dialogue, surfacing hidden issues and creating an environment for team learning. The ability to facilitate a group is not only an essential skill of consulting, but a capability that must be taught to many of the key leaders within the company.

Facilitation means watching and intervening in the process of the group (how it works), rather than its content (what it is doing). It is helping a group operate as a non-hierarchical, collaborative body, and teaching the group members how to facilitate—to transfer that capability to the client. This teaching is especially important in the Change Team.

The facilitator is not the leader of the group. The facilitator is the teacher and creator of the group's container—its working environment. Leadership and facilitation are often at cross-purposes: the leader has a task and outcome orientation, while the facilitator has a process orientation. A group can, and often does, have both a leader and a facilitator. It is rarely appropriate for the Change Navigator to be the Group or Team Leader, because they are not accountable or responsible for outcomes.

5. Team Development

Much of the Change Navigator's work is done through the vehicle of gathering a team. They have the dual role of helping the team learn to be a team, and offering some of their expert knowledge about how to create change.

The group needs to learn how to become a group and how to create an effective process, before it can begin its business:

- Groups have internal processes, ways of operating, and roles and assumptions that can help or get in the way of its task

- There is often a set of unspoken assumptions and processes that inhibit the group from achieving its aim

- The Navigator helps the group uncover obstacles to its agenda and get back on track, by illuminating the process to the group and helping the group design alternatives

Setting up an effective change process involves two dimensions:

- Creating a shared model of what will be done

- Building a team of leaders within the organization as partners in getting it done

The roadmap or plan needs to be owned by the key people in the organization, not just the leadership, before they will understand and commit to the process.

The Navigator works primarily with a Change Team within the organization, and the process, model, and means of creating change must be agreed upon. The Navigator acts as convenor/facilitator of the cross-functional Change Team that will own the change process, and deal with some of the political and cultural obstacles that sometimes accompany such design processes.

The Change Teams encounter a fundamental paradox of real change: to offer a process that is congruent with the basic culture of the organization, but also that challenges some aspects of the status quo and traditional ways of doing business.

The process of design is as important as facilitation:

- It begins by learning and planning with representatives who will share the responsibility for the outcome

- The process must facilitate the group's objectives, and utilize good process technology and tools

- It should have clear, explicit outcomes and action steps

- It is collaborative, and involves shared leadership and coaching

SUSTAINING THE COURSE—IT'S THE PEOPLE

Organizations experiencing change are stressful and difficult places to be. Daily operations must continue, while at the same time a new path is being created. There is no way to stop and start over again. In effect, change is an additional responsibility that is added to operational tasks. At the same time, everything is up in the air.

Uncertainty Is the Outcome

The experience of an organization during change is one of uncertainty and confusion. While we seem to be offering an orderly course, the map is not the territory itself. The orderly course usually feels confused and incomplete. Even as the leaders feel they are informing people, people will not feel they know enough to change. The outcome of any change is by definition uncertain, as people are leaving behind the predictable past for the uncertain future. Some people will not be able to take up the challenge and they will have to step aside. As many people are involved in change, the potential for conflict and working at cross-purposes is heightened. People will begin to idealize the "good old days" while they find themselves resisting the new. The leaders of the change—in roles such as that of Sponsor, Change Leaders, Change Team members and Change Navigators—will have to work diligently to bring each person on board the moving ship.

Effective change does not occur when people are told to change and obey, but when the people in the organization learn new ways and develop a commitment to them. It is a difficult process because the organization often needs new skill sets to go in a new direction. The uncertainty of change can become highly upsetting when individuals are wondering if there is a place for them, while the organization wants them to focus on making the organization successful. Change Leaders must face the reality that people need to solve their personal dilemma before they can come on board to help the organization change.

Challenges of Moving People Through Change

Change takes longer and demands more resources and work than most leaders would like. People have difficulty with change, and when the organization changes its processes, systems, or structure, sometimes people don't complete the change. We see the following outcomes of poorly managed change:

- ■ *Not everyone has really signed up to take the company into a major new direction.* The organization needs to make a major shift to remain viable. A major product or service line has matured and there are no new ones on the horizon. A new competitor or technology offers a threat. The company has merged with another, but initially, employees and management are too tied to the old ways to make the changes needed to remain competitive in the future— threatening the long-term future of the company because they don't understand or have the skills to be effective in the emerging work environment.

- ■ *Process designs and other changes do not get implemented or do not achieve the desired results.* Employees do not continue to implement new designs after the original initiators leave. They don't really understand why they needed to change, or how critical the change is to the future of the company. The change effort is aborted, and the organization wants to regain its momentum.

- ■ *Employees become burned out and apathetic, and morale plummets after a downsizing, new initiative or other major change.* Managers report that productivity and morale have bottomed out after the change. They want to get employees remotivated, and recommitted to the new work environment.

■ *Following major shifts (mergers, re-locations, etc.), new leaders don't help employees understand, accept and thrive in a new culture, values or work environment.* Leaders report that they don't know how to get people to accept the changes. Productivity and morale plummet before or after the transition, because people need to understand the new directions, and need help to become part of the new entity.

■ *Change is initiated before important parts of the organization are ready to change or still have strong, hidden reservations about it.* There may be important information bearing on the change that is not utilized, which will affect the results or outcome. *Organizational change is changing people.*

Sustaining Change

The major dilemma about the changes that organizations need is that people change differently than systems. Systems don't talk back, they don't question, and they don't have feelings. Change theorist Gregory Bateson talked about the difference between kicking a tree and kicking a dog. Both people and systems are designed to maintain themselves, which means they have difficulty changing. We are all familiar with changes that acted like rubberbands—springing back to the old way after a short period. The problems of change involve creating change that is sustainable and that is deep enough to cause the people in the organization as well as the system to change.

When we observed organizations that struggled with change, their concerns were always the same—how can we get people to change:

- How can all the people within the organization get mobilized so that they will understand, accept and participate in the process of change?

- How can organizations get people to actually implement changes that are well conceived?

- What can be done to regain commitment and productivity after the change has happened?

- How can people learn not just to accept a change, but to initiate and work within an organization that is capable of continual change?

For change to be sustainable within the organization, both people and systems need to change:

- People need to learn before they can change their behavior. People need commitment to the change, and they need the skills and capabilities to accomplish the new tasks. They need to learn and to change their expectations, mindsets, and assumptions about what is important, and how they get things done.

- The organization needs clear direction, alignment of efforts and integration of different strands of the change.

What leaders think will be a simple change can become complex and much more difficult than expected.

To achieve real change, each employee, and also each team, work group and the organization as a whole, must go through a process leading to an informed, effective and aligned commitment to the changes and the desired outcome. This commitment develops through several phases:

Pathways to Developing Commitment	
Question	**Response**
1. Awareness "Why?"	Information
2. Capability "How?"	Skill Development
3. Commitment "Who?"	Participation
4. Alignment "What?"	Collaborative Design

Key Principles of Change

To develop a committed workforce in a change-capable organization, certain principles must be observed in the change effort.

Change Is Learning How to Learn

Change represents much more than making a single change; this is a first-order change. Effective change is a second-order change, meaning that it is a change in the way the organization approaches change. It is about developing the capacity to learn and grow as an organization, an expansion of the capabilities of the organization, especially the capabilities of managing change.

Change Is People Learning and Using New Skills and Capabilities

The core of effective change is a learning process among the people in the organization. This is different than developing a model or plan for the organization because the change is internal, within people. It shows up in changed relationships, systems and work processes, but the major shift is internal. Change is rooted in a model of learning and skill development. Therefore, many of the activities for effective change consist of learning events for groups of people, focused on skill development and change.

Effective Change Comes from Relationships, Not Information

People learn about change through relationships. Relationship elements such as trust, credibility, congruence between words and actions, sharing of relevant information, developmental coaching and teaching of relevant skills form the cornerstone of change management. The organization learns not from what the leader or consultant says, but by the power of the example of what they do.

In order to change, people need both information and relationship:

- Information engages the rational side of the person, providing the what, why and how of a change

- Relationship engages the emotional side of the person, offering support, participation, and involvement in the change

Change Leaders need to offer the people in their organization both information and relationship. Relationship allows you to walk the line between challenge and support, and between focusing attention on important information.

Change Must Occur at Multiple Levels

Deep, meaningful change must be initiated simultaneously at different levels of the organization. Every organization has a visible level of behavior, structures, policies and systems which everyone acknowledges and follows. But below this lies a level of what has been called the "culture of the organization," which contains basic values and assumptions that people make about how they should be doing things and what they expect. If a change affects the visible layer but does not also change the culture, the likelihood is that the culture will cause the organization to begin to spring back to the old ways. Too many times, we have seen organizations change their information systems or performance management systems without also shifting their values and assumptions about how people should behave. In the traditional culture, every manager tried to keep his or her group's information from other groups, and even though the new information systems centralized access to information, the group continued to sit on its results by not entering them on the new system in a timely manner.

To change deeply, an organization needs its employees and managers to:

- See why they have to change
- Let go of old ways
- Align with the new direction
- Adapt their values and behavior with the new ways
- Commit to what needs to be done to make it work
- Be active in creating success
- Learn new skills and mindsets
- Be ready for more change in the future

All of this will not happen if people are simply told that they have to change.

INITIATING A CHANGE—GETTING STARTED

Change must start somewhere. Someone in the organization gets the idea or sees a need or an opportunity for change. Someone sees a threat, danger, or change in the environment, and realizes that the organization must respond.

An internal (or external) organizational leader can become a Change Leader, initiating change in the organization by:

- Defining change/leadership priorities and options

- Presenting change leadership perspectives, possibilities and processes to the organization

- Planning and integrating change leadership efforts within a broader change initiative

First Steps in Change

Before you set off on a change initiative take some time to:

- Think through your purposes

- Create a high-level design with a strategic illustration to focus your activities

A sequence of three activities will get you started:

1. Getting out and talking informally to key stakeholders

2. Thoughtful planning and defining of your efforts

3. Sharing your initial thoughts with many people inside and outside the organization, to acquaint them with your idea and get their feedback

The purpose of this initial reflection process is to help you creatively explore the possibilities and create a climate where change can begin.

The organization is not yet ready to change. It is invested in the way it does things today. As a Change Leader or Navigator, you are a prophet. You want to lead the organization to a vision of a better way, not continue the status quo. Prior to starting your change leadership efforts, you need to introduce change to key decision makers in the organization:

- To build understanding of what change entails

- To get their active support and involvement for your efforts

Your presentation of the need for change will be critical for getting the organization to commit the necessary energy, leadership, resources and people to the efforts. There are several ways that you can do this:

- Informal conversations

- Participating as a change leadership resource on project teams

- Making change leadership presentations to different groups

Framing Questions to Begin Initiating Change

A series of framing questions will help you create a preliminary change leadership roadmap to engage the leadership of the organization or business unit to support a potential change. The questions will help you conduct your own exploration, your own due diligence, leading you to decide whether to commit your credibility and influence to initiating change in your organization.

Answer the following questions as best you can. Your responses form a guide to seek greater clarity about each one, as you negotiate your involvement:

#1   Why should we change?
#2   What or how should we change?
#3   What are its change leadership challenges?
#4   What is the focus of the change leadership efforts?
#5   How will change leadership activities help achieve the desired changes, business results, and enhanced capability?
#6   How can we mobilize support in this effort?
#7   What resources are available?
#8   What boundaries must we cross?

Question #1: Why should we change?

What are the external triggers that alert us to the need to change? You must gather the evidence to make the case to change. This data will then be used to make the case for the change throughout the organization.

An external change is not enough reason to mobilize an organization for major change. You must gather evidence of why there is no alternative, and the consequences of not changing. The search for data will bring you into contact with people in the organization who help answer these questions. They will later become key supporters of change. You should use this first question to help you recruit key internal supporters to the effort.

Question #2: What or how should we change?

Define clearly the changes that the organization desires to produce in the overall change initiative. Supporting these changes will always be the focus of your activity.

Every change has three aspects:

- What leaders want to change in the organization

- The business results they expect from the change

- The ways that the change will enhance their organizational capacity

You should define these goals not simply from the public statement, but validate and expand upon it through conversations with clients and the members of your consulting team.

Question #3: What are its change leadership challenges?

What do you see as the potential change management implications or issues that creating this sort of change will raise in the organization?

Your response should combine your own experience and intuitions with the concerns you discover from talks with other people in the organization.

Make these implications concrete and specific:

For example, instead of   "Employees will have to accept the change."

You might write: "Information Systems employees are very committed
to the legacy system and are reluctant to change to a
client-server system," or "From past history, people
feel changes will not really be made."

Challenges also include organizational norms—the way they do things and the behavior they expect from employees, that might inhibit change efforts:

"We don't question our managers," or "We don't rock the boat."

"We do things through established channels," or "We don't take action on our
own initiative."

You should learn about past history of dealing with change, especially past failures or scars from unsuccessful change efforts which affect the next effort.

Question #4: What is the focus of the change leadership efforts?

Change leadership means many things to different people. Use this question to make sure that you and other members of your client and consulting team are using the same language.

Some of the ways to approach this question include asking:

- How do the different leadership groups in the organization see and define the need for change?

- What do you suggest in the area of change leadership?

- What does the organization need that they feel change can provide? If they are cautious, what are their key concerns?

- What specific change initiatives should the organization consider?

- Will the change effort be oriented primarily toward:

  —Supporting some other change initiative
  —Achieving a change initiative set by the company
  —Building positive support for other proposed difficult changes
  —Overcoming or diffusing anticipated resistance to change

Question #5: How will change leadership activities help the client achieve the desired changes, business results, and enhanced capability?

Detail the specific changes you expect that change leadership will provide to the organization and how they will impact the proposed organizational change.

State the desired changes in terms of what will change in relation to:

- People

- The Organization—including its systems for managing people

Note why these outcomes are important to the success of the overall change initiative.

Question #6: How can we mobilize support in this effort?

Generally, the success of change initiatives hinges on building strong partnerships with a few key people in the organization. These may be your formal contacts, for example, the director of human resources or corporate communication, or they may be informal leaders, people who have access to resources or who are concerned about elements of the change, and who can help in your efforts.

You will need to seek out people who hold the three crucial roles in relation to any change effort:

- ■ **Sponsors:** Define clearly who in the organization is accountable for the results of the change. This is the sponsor of the effort. You need to build a strong relationship with your sponsors.

- ■ **Change Leaders/Project Managers:** The people who will actually carry out different elements of the change. They have operational or management responsibility for a change effort.

■ ***Stakeholders, Champions and Other Key Influencers:*** Next you need to seek the change champions, key people who are excited about change who will be affected by the change, and who want to be part of, or are visible and vocal potential supporters of your effort, and build relationships with them. Define who these people might be and reach out to them from the start of your efforts.

Question #7: What resources are available?

The extent of your effort is related to the resources available to you. If your effort is to have the desired impact, you need to work within the resources you have, or make a case for more resources early in the process.

Look for resources including:

- The personnel who are formally available to the project and the degree of their availability

- Informal resources who can assist you in your work, such as activities you can piggyback on (such as an internal communications campaign)

- The degree of funding available for communication, navigation and involvement

If the resources are not reasonable to achieve the desired outcomes, you need to address this issue early enough to lobby for more commitment.

Question #8: What boundaries must we cross?

Throughout the change leadership process you need to be aware of and define the boundary conditions and anticipate the challenges and pitfalls you might face. The earlier you anticipate them, the more you can prepare to overcome them effectively.

Look for potential obstacles and constraints on your work in areas such as:

- Core values that may conflict
- Budget limitations
- Time and schedule deadlines
- Limitations of scope of your efforts (put in the form of "don't touch this," or "don't address this issue")

- Sacred cows—things that you are told (formally or implicitly) are off limits or undiscussable (like executive compensation)

- Current legacy systems (in human resources or information services) or practices that the company has invested in that are difficult to change

- Sources of pain or current crisis that make it difficult to change

You need to be aware of these boundaries in order to overcome them. You may have to challenge some of these limits if they undermine the organization's ability to create real, sustainable change.

ORGANIZATIONAL CHANGE WAVES

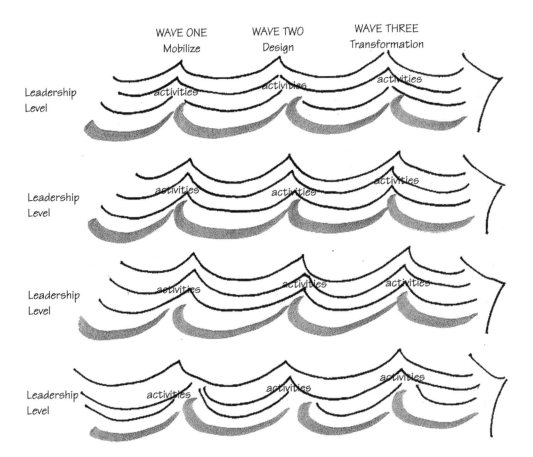

Each section that follows explains the principles and key activity by each level of the organization to guide it through the process of transformational change. Each section contains the following "architecture."

Setting the Course

Challenges

Guiding Principles

Activities

Navigation Tool

Wave One

MOBILIZING THE ORGANIZATION FOR CHANGE

Key Tasks

- *Align Top Leadership*
- *Convene and Charter the Change Team*
- *Develop Individual Change Capability*
- *Assess Organizational Change Capability*

WAVE ONE: INTRODUCTION

The first wave involves mobilizing the whole organization for the complex and difficult process of changing. Mobilizing is much more than getting the go-ahead for a change initiative, or getting managers to agree to it. It involves the entire organization understanding why they have to change and what change will mean for them. It means getting people ready to take up their roles in the change and sharing the responsibility for its success.

In the first wave, the whole organization decides that it will change and commits to a shared path. Design of the change itself is not yet the organization's focus. Before that can happen, the tasks of Wave One create the processes and structures for the process of design itself. This involves aligning top leadership around the change, convening a cross-functional Change Team and mobilizing the whole organization to become involved in change. The organization doesn't yet know where change will take them, but they are clear about the general outlines of their direction and the need for change. In Wave One, the organization initiates a shared pathway to change. For this process to succeed, different levels and roles need to understand, commit to, and get ready for change.

The two primary outcomes of the first wave are:

- Engaging everyone in the organization to accept responsibility for the change

- Defining the tasks and roles for key groups in the change process

The four key tasks of Wave One are overlapping, but sequential. They contain the activities, responsibilities and outcomes that concern each level of the organization. Each group needs to understand its unique role and contribution to the change effort. They describe a circular process, where every element of the organization is engaged in anticipating change from their own perspective and then integrating their efforts into the whole.

In organizations that are not destined to succeed at change, these activities are often given only lip service. Change efforts all too frequently begin with people jumping into doing and planning, rather than mobilizing the organization's awareness and general capability for change. This aligning period does not lengthen the overall time for change or add to its cost. Rather, change efforts that neglect this up-front mobilization either fail to generate commitment, or have to invest later, taking more time and at a greater cost.

The four key tasks of Wave One are:

TASK 1: ALIGN TOP LEADERSHIP

The leadership needs to get beyond their individual interests, and align around the proposed change. They need to understand the costs and potential benefits of the change and agree to support them. They need to make the commitment to being active and visible in helping the organization change. The leaders set the parameters for change—the need, the general direction or strategic intention of change, and the context for the design and implementation of the change. They don't prescribe the solutions or the whole path.

TASK 2: CONVENE AND CHARTER THE CHANGE TEAM

The Change Team is a group representing all parts of the organization that will be changing. It is a powerful group, not of the top tier, but consisting of up-and-coming leaders who want to make a difference. This group takes on a huge responsibility—to design and steer the change. They are chartered by the top leaders to make the change happen. They link the top leaders with the rest of the organization.

TASK 3: DEVELOP INDIVIDUAL CHANGE CAPABILITY

The employees are the people who change. Effective change efforts can't just tell people to change. They must understand about the need to change so that they can prepare to change, and they must develop both the skills and the understanding of what is happening, so that they can take up their new roles. The employees need to be involved in the initiation of change, and must begin to develop new skills as quickly as possible.

TASK 4: ASSESS ORGANIZATIONAL CHANGE CAPABILITY

Before beginning to change the Sponsors, Change Leaders, Change Navigators and Change Team have to develop a good sense of how able and competent the organization is about change. The organizational capability assessment is more than data gathering, it involves various parts of the organization beginning to look at how ready they are for change.

The first step, aligning top leadership around change is detailed in Task 1.

TASK 1: ALIGN TOP LEADERSHIP

Key Activities

 ■ *Initiate Change*

 ■ *Charter Leaders and Navigator*

 ■ *Set Strategic Direction for Change*

SETTING THE COURSE

Why should we change? That is the basic question the top leaders of an organization or business unit must answer before change can proceed. But agreement on the need to change is only the start. Then, the top leaders must come to agreement on the scope of the change and the remedy. And finally, if they agree on what to change, then they must agree on the role they will play to make the change successful. Disagreement at the start can only lead to confusion or working at cross-purposes later on.

The first step in change is for the initiator of the change, whether a member of the leadership team, even the CEO, or a visionary leader at a level below the top team, to develop top leadership commitment and alignment around the change. The activities here include making the full case for change to the executive team, helping them understand the costs and implications of the proposed change and working with them to develop alignment around the change.

Core Activities	**Outcomes**

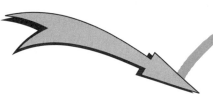

- Get high-level commitment

- Define the roles and responsibilities of the Sponsor and the Change Navigator

- Reach clarity and agreement among the leadership team concerning implications and consequences of the change

- Commitment for significant organizational engagement

- Excitement and understanding about the change initiative among the members of the executive team

- Understand implications of the change for the organization

- Link change with the business vision

- Clarity and commitment about leadership role

CHALLENGES

Learning How To Lead Change

Leaders often do not have the skills needed to lead change. They also do not know that they do not have these skills, because people in the organization are not willing to tell them.

Leaders are often experienced in day-to-day operations, but inexperienced in leading change and taking an organization in radically new directions. The Leadership Team needs to understand that leading change demands a different role and style of leadership. The leaders need to learn what typically happens during large-scale change and what it demands in terms of executive leadership. They are used to planning and controlling change; whereas change in a turbulent environment needs leaders who set the direction and context for change and then step back and let the whole organization evolve under the direction of Change Leaders, Navigators and Teams.

The executive team is concerned with strategic integration of the new direction, in the actions of every person in the organization. It has high visibility, being watched by all in the organization. Its visibility magnifies the impact of political dynamics among members.

Changing Leader Behavior

It is not easy to evoke or stabilize new behavior in large numbers of employees who are often anxious or upset by the changes. Changing habits or creating new ones is one of the toughest parts of making change stick, long-term.

Change demands new behaviors for managing employee feelings and motivation:

- Developing and communicating a simple vision

- Creating a need for change in people's minds and hearts by simultaneously showing the extent of what is possible and today's reality

- Confronting colleagues when they are not supporting the change

- Facing up to people's expressions of negativity

- Mediating strong conflict among key people in the organization

- Allowing people at lower levels in the organization freedom to discover their own way to align with the new direction

Whole System Focus

Ssuccessful change calls for a systemic approach, developing the whole picture of the nature and implications of the change before starting to change parts of the organization. The tendency of most organizations is to segment functions and responsibilities, creating simultaneous initiatives, quality programs and training. This confuses people, particularly those lower in the organization. They do what they are told but they do not understand why or how far to go, and feel like they are following a "whichever way the wind blows" program rather than really changing.

Is it essential to create a focused understanding of what is changing and why. But without a systemic approach, it is quite difficult to do so. With a systemic approach, people learn how to look for interrelationships and address issues where there is the greatest leverage. Top executives frequently embody turf battles. If a cross-functional change initiative is to stand any chance, the top leaders have to agree to set aside some of their politics to achieve organizational goals.

Sponsorship Is Active

Initially, the leadership team is not clearly aligned and ready to take responsibility for the change. The Change Sponsor is the executive who perceives the need for change and has the power to influence the whole organization or organizational unit. The sponsor stands up and says, "We will do this." The Change Sponsor may or may not be the CEO or President. He or she does not necessarily drive the change personally, but he or she gets it to happen. But the rest of the leadership team needs to support and align their efforts with the change as well. It cannot be delegated to one executive alone. The political, power and turf issues between the sponsor and the rest of the team must be addressed up-front and openly.

The sponsor's role is to provide security and support for the person given the job of driving the change project. The challenge involves developing a collaborative relationships, sustaining the right "tension and attention" in the organization throughout the change, and building others' understanding and commitment.

Alignment

Misalignment occurs when the senior team is not willing to spend the time and energy working the alignment and change management issues, or key members of the team or board don't support the change. For change to succeed, the executives need to get below the superficial agreement that often covers up fundamental misalignment.

This requires open discussion of authority, role, refocused intent and resource allocation. However, if not addressed, these issues can blow the change effort apart or cause it to die a slow death.

Expect Disruption

Even successful change can feel as though it is tearing the organization apart—and the leaders are the ones responsible. Since this is generally not an acceptable thing to discuss or even feel, it does not get addressed. These "dark side" issues such as loss, grief, re-creation of identity and disruption of habit and assumptions often cause people to mislead themselves about how long things will take or how difficult they will be. Learning how to talk about the these experiences can be critical to sustaining people's commitment.

GUIDING PRINCIPLES

■ *The Change Sponsor and executive team must collectively own (e.g., be fully accountable for the success of) the change initiative.* Unless they do, they will not resource it adequately or lend their personal, visible commitment to it. It is unlikely to succeed without their commitment. If the change initiative is perceived as a staff-led or consultant-led project, it is set up for failure.

■ *Go for the real change that is needed—not just the symptoms.* The leadership needs to face reality. If the change is merely addressing symptoms, it will not resolve the underlying problems. Usually people throughout an organization know the main problems, but there has been no opportunity to address them. It is critical that the leaders face up to the real nature of the problems up-front. This may mean more time for diagnosis than they are comfortable with, and spending more time listening to the organization before they initiate action.

■ *Lead change, don't control it.* The leaders should try to hold off telling the organization how to change or what to change, and focus on setting a strategic direction and desired outcomes. This will involve delegating the process of change to a Change Team and trusting them to design the change with the organization.

■ *Set a strategic direction.* Bring vision to the situation. Ensure that there is a powerful, clear, compelling vision for the future, including both business viability and sustaining (or creating) a work environment valued by the range of people needed for success. They need to hold off from prescribing the how, and focus on getting everyone to work on the process, to produce the best possible new direction.

■ *Encourage in-depth dialogue, even when leaders are initially uncomfortable.* Executive team members must openly share their reservations as well as their desires regarding the change initiative in order to craft one that will be successful. In dealing with their unexpressed fears they need to seek the right depth for communication. When communication is not deep or complete enough, either the real issues go unrecognized or unanticipated blow-ups occur.

KEY ACTIVITIES FOR TASK 1

ACTIVITY 1: Initiate Change

Someone in the organization wants to change. This person, sometimes an unsung hero, is the real initiator of the change. It can be a top executive, or a person one or even several levels below. They have done their homework, and gathered the information about the need for the type of change they propose. The task now is to bring this information to the top team and have them act on it. This is the beginning of change.

The Change Initiator may first try out the proposal with some potential champions, influential people, or important advocates to get their buy-in before making the case. The more people that the initiator involves in the idea generation, the easier the change will be. There may also have been some limited innovation by the Change Initiator in his or her work team or business unit. The request then is to move the change process more widely through the organization.

Here are some of the activities the Change Initiator will undertake:

- Talking to people around the company about the need for change and possible pathways

- Gathering relevant information from throughout the organization (e.g., customer data, market information, technical need)

- Offering briefings and bringing in experts and others who might help the organization understand the need for the change

- Getting support from informal leaders and champions around the organization

- Talking to the people who will be most affected, or who might feel that they will lose out in the change, to try to find ways to include them

- Commit yourself fully to being an initiator

If the proposal generates or uncovers conflict among the main members of the executive group, the team must resolve these issues before they can mobilize the organization for change. If the executives are divided, the layers below will sense that and feel confused around whether or what to change.

The outcome will be that the Change Initiator makes his or her case to the executive team, and they either agree to go ahead or ask for more time or information to consider.

ACTIVITY 2: Charter Leaders and Navigator

In order to begin a change, the Leadership Team must now name and empower Change Leaders and a Change Navigator. This Change Team is delegated the responsibility for the change. It is critical that the Executive Team understand that they are the Change Sponsors, not the people who carry out change. Some top teams try to lead the change themselves, or do not really allow others to become change leaders. Too frequently, they do not have a Change Navigator either. This leads to the leadership getting overwhelmed and many tasks not getting done.

The Change Leader and Navigator meet with the Change Sponsor(s) to discuss their relative roles in the change initiative and ensure agreement about the overall plans. It is critical to map out the process and ensure that the sponsor and change leaders see eye-to-eye. This can take several meetings, and may include the first of many change retreats—where selected members of the top team, and those to whom the change is delegated, work together to define the key strategic parameters of the change. The outcome of this task should be a formal written charter of what will be done generally outlining the purposes and desired outcomes, the available resources, and the deliverables and expectations. This is too important not to be written down, and the charter will then be available to the Change Team and other groups involved in change to set the direction.

The Change Navigator then plans and implements the rest of the key tasks of major change initiatives:

- Convene and charter Change Team (Task 2)

- Develop Individual Change Capability (Task 3)

- Assess Organizational Change Capability (Task 4)

ACTIVITY 3: Set Strategic Direction For Change

With the Change Leader and Navigator on board, the Executive Team comes together at a series of workshops and sets the broad strategic direction of the organization in light of changing environmental conditions. They may include other relevant people from the organization—sometimes a strategic direction process is similar to the large group events that we will discuss under **Employee Involvement Process** (page 115). Until this is done, any change runs the risk of being the wrong response. Too many changes involve doing good things, but not ones that resolve or overcome the issues that led to the change. Organizations are in effect charting the wrong course. The strategic direction, or vision, is not the complete plan for change. It is the overall course of where the company wants to go, why it must go, and some general indications of how to get there. The specific plan will come from other places and involve many more people.

Setting strategic direction has been the subject of many books. It is important to note that setting the direction is not the same as the change itself, or even the plan to change. Setting the strategic direction should include:

- Gathering data from the market, competitive analysis, and trends that define why the organization needs to change and the urgency of it

- Setting big goals that inspire and challenge the organization

- Defining or clarifying the values of the organization, will hold to as they navigate the change

- Making clear the different levels of responsibility for change, and the priority of the change process

NAVIGATION TOOL:
LEADERSHIP ALIGNMENT RETREAT

Before change can be mandated, even if the CEO decides it is important, the Executive Team must go through a process of alignment and chartering of the change. The basic tool for achieving this will be a **Leadership Alignment Retreat**. This retreat usually needs an outside person to facilitate it, because the leaders must focus on working together. The facilitator of the retreat can be the internal Change Navigator, but more frequently, this is a key task for an outside consultant, who is independent of the organization. Such a person can effectively challenge the executives without fear of his or her job, and can bring in an outside perspective on how change happens at other organizations. This retreat is a collaborative event among the Change Navigator, the Change Sponsor, and top executives. It is a working session intended to ensure sufficient alignments and excitement among the members of the Executive Team to provide a solid foundation for success of the change project. This is an intensive off-site workshop that is held at the beginning of the change initiative, with the goal of creating an effective leadership team to lead the organization to successful change.

The purpose of the workshop is to:

- Ensure alignment among the members of the executive team

- Help the members of the Leadership Team picture what they will have to do differently in order for the project to be successful

- Plan for the work of the Change Team

It should be designed in conjunction with the Change Sponsor, who will be making it clear that he or she supports the process. It is held offsite because this signifies that people take it seriously enough to schedule time away from their other work in order to attend to it. It is important to record the thought process of the group and to record all decisions.

The executives must then convene and charter the Change Team. This ensures commonalty of vision and intention between these two key teams, and an effective hand-off of responsibility. This workshop will serve to clarify and negotiate any outstanding details of their respective roles in the Change Initiative, as well as develop a common understanding of the dynamics of change.

TASK 2: CONVENE AND CHARTER THE CHANGE TEAM

Key Activities

- *Recruit and Charter Change Team*

- *Team Designs How They Will Work Together*

SETTING THE COURSE

The first change the organization must undertake is to select, train and develop the team to lead the change. Change does not take place using normal pathways or normal channels of the organization. Change represents an upheaval to the way things are done. In order for an organization to initiate change, it must create what is called a "parallel organization," a special cross-functional, multi-level group of empowered leaders, to whom the Leadership Team and Sponsor dele-gates the task and some of the responsibility for designing the process of change. This is usually an entirely new type of team and role for the organization. The organization usually does not already have a Change Team in place. This section will help you designate the right people for this role.

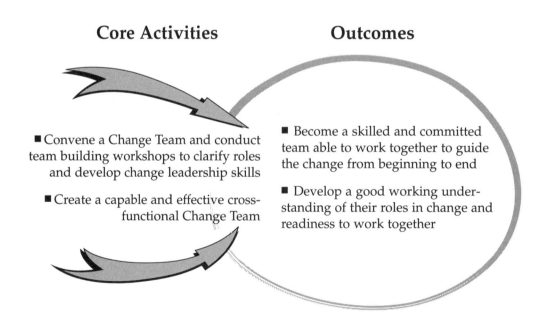

Core Activities

■ Convene a Change Team and conduct team building workshops to clarify roles and develop change leadership skills

■ Create a capable and effective cross-functional Change Team

Outcomes

■ Become a skilled and committed team able to work together to guide the change from beginning to end

■ Develop a good working understanding of their roles in change and readiness to work together

CHALLENGES

Define Role, Responsibility and Team Charter

From the moment it is designated, the Change Team becomes a powerful new group of leaders in the organization. They have an enormous task, and are delegated decision authority for many elements of change. They are sometimes unclear about the extent of their authority and what exactly they are supposed to accomplish. The organization needs to create a process for them to be clear about what they are doing.

The new team must spend time up-front understanding their charter from the leadership, and developing clear role definition for this unfamiliar and highly consequential role. They need to come to agreement concerning:

- Their team charter (mission of team, boundary between Change Team and Leadership Team)

- The role of the team leader, team members and facilitator/consultant. There is a high likelihood for role confusion or conflict for most major changes. It is important that the consultant and Change Team Leader clarify their respective roles.

- A clear set of responsibilities for who will:

  —Educate the organization

  —Anticipate and manage resistance

  —Address difficult issues along the way

  —Guide the process

The organization, even the people in the Change Team, may never have really done any change, and the organization may not have supported previous change efforts. The Change Team needs to learn how to lead change, and it should be absolutely clear to them that this will mean doing things the organization has not done before. They may also have to overcome a negative history of frustrated or poorly implemented change. In addition, they need to learn how to do these things, and they need support and coaching to set them into action. They must be clear and aligned over doing this, and support each other as well.

Represent the Rest of the Organization, Don't Become Isolated from It

Once people are named to the Change Team, they run the risk of losing touch and losing the trust of their peers on the job. Isolation sets in, despite their best intentioned efforts. Change Team membership is a highly visible and often a prestigious and misunderstood role. The rest of the organization needs to receive a clear understanding of their role and be asked to support their work. They need to take care to keep in touch with their original teams, even as they develop a new perspective.

Making Tough Decisions

The Change Team is faced with a difficult task—often to accomplish the seemingly impossible, with limited resources and a tight timeframe. They have to overcome and challenge some of the traditional, even successful ways of the organization and challenge vested interests and roles. They may not be sure of their own job security or future.

The members of the Change Team have to be selected for courage and ability to set a new path, as well as being trusted and respected by peers. They will have to be courageous and tough, because they are following a mandate of the leaders to raise the bar—to move forward into uncertain, risky territory. They will have to challenge people in power, do things that are highly unpopular and act despite conflict. They will need special support for this role. They should be selected for their personal skills and ability to set direction for others, rather than follow the current tide.

GUIDING PRINCIPLES

■ *The Change Team must represent all the functional groups and levels of the organization.* In choosing the right people for the team, use the following principles to guide choice—ownership, commitment, representation, and information-flow. The team should be cross-functional and multi-level. It should contain mostly people committed to the change, along with some skeptics on the team—but not cynics.

■ *Ensure that clear roles and responsibilities exist for and between each person, and the team as a whole.* The Change Team must be very clear about their roles and responsibilities. They have been given or participated in setting the strategic direction and some large challenges, but they are given the freedom, and the burden, of deciding how to do this. The Leadership Team will have to give them the resources and authority to do the task, which will be defined as the Change Team sets it course. They are responsible for the process: for designing and implementing the change. They share accountability for the outcomes with the leadership team.

■ *Invest time in building consensus and alignment between the key influencers and teams.* Too often the team will drive hard to get a decision, bypassing important differences of opinion along the way. The effect is a rapid decision, but little alignment among team members for the decision. True alignment among team members cannot occur without some "sweat and blood." Alignment between the Change Team, the Leadership Team and the rest of the organization is equally critical. Spending the time to create a shared vision and plan for the change process is the best way to gain alignment.

■ *Encourage trust through a full and timely disclosure of information.* There is a tendency for Change Teams and leaders to hoard information. There is a natural tendency not to share information, plans, work-in-progress or decisions until they are clear and complete. Yet people feel insecure as a result of the lack of information. They also feel less in control as a result of limited information, while the Change Team feels more in control. More than anything else, people need to feel and have control by knowing what is going on. Therefore, full disclosure throughout the organization at each step along the way is preferable to little information.

The most compelling reason to share information is that absence of it breeds mistrust while the presence of it builds trust. Trust will be the most critical element in the process of change. There also needs to be opportunities for all members of the organization to communicate to the Change Team, for it is through this communication that the Change Team keeps a pulse on the organization.

KEY ACTIVITIES FOR TASK 2

ACTIVITY 1: Recruit and Charter Change Team

The Change Leader, Navigator and Sponsor or Leadership Team select from 6–12 members of the Change Team. For a major change they should be more that 50 percent and ideally 100 percent dedicated to this task. It has to be their major role. The team should represent the key groups who will be changed. The people on the team should be a mix of informal and formal leaders of the business unit or groups that are changing. Select people who are seen as up-and-coming, with new ideas, high energy, trusted by others, and with high levels of influence skills.

Each Change Team member commits to long-term membership, and ongoing efforts for education on the process and human dynamics of change. When they sign on they must be fully informed of what they are being asked to do. They will have some concerns about their future roles, job security, return to their original team or reassignment, and rewards for service which should be faced by the Change Sponsor up-front. Not clarifying these factors can lead to lower levels of commitment and lack of engagement of the Change Team. The change charter that has been drafted by the Leadership Team, Change Leader and Navigator is shared with this team. The Change Leader will usually be the leader of the Change Team, in that they report to him or her, but often the Change Leader, unlike the rest of the team, has operational responsibilities in the unit that is changing. The Change Navigator is often the leader of the Change Team, working full-time on the project. But the scope of each of these roles needs to be clear.

ACTIVITY 2: Team Designs How They Will Work Together

Initiate the team building process as soon as possible. Some part of the workshop should include the Change Sponsor and members of the leadership, both to inspire the Change Team as well as to ensure that all key players are in alignment with one another going forward. The result of this is a strong sense of urgency that will guide the motivation for change.

The members of the team need to be willing to take on this responsibility and all the successes and frustrations that go along with it. For this, the spirit of relationship between people within each role and between groups needs to be clear.

NAVIGATION TOOL:
TEAM-BUILDING WORKSHOP

Soon after it is named, the Change Team should get together for an off-site retreat for from 2–5 days. This retreat should be considered as a crash education course in change leadership, combined with a process of coming together as a team, defining how they will work and building a shared sense of commitment and direction.

The following activities are essential for this workshop:

- Clarify the team's purpose (reason for existence), and become deeply grounded in the reasons for the change. This often involves a deep understanding of the industry, the changes in the industry and in the business community, and the implications of those changes on the organization as a whole. The team must have all the information necessary to understand as fully as the Leadership Team why the organization must change, and the reasons for the new strategic direction.

- Identify what must be accomplished:

  —Goals and objectives

  —Key deliverables

  —Timelines

- Explore what is known about the change process and what they need to learn in order to accomplish their job

- Define the roles and responsibilities of the Change Team, Change Navigator and Change Leader, and between Change Team and top leadership

- Define how to engage the whole organization and report on their activities

- Agree on expectations of the team members including:

  —Who does what—role clarity

  —Commitments needed (e.g., key outcomes—sponsor behaviors)

  —Team behaviors and attitudes—ground rules

- Deal with team members issues, concerns and resistances to change

    —Clarify skills and competencies needed going forward

    —Help team members take responsibility for change

    —Provide development plan to support team members in their growth as they lead change

Learn about Change

The change that the team undertakes can only be as broad and deep and comprehensive as their understanding. The Change Team members are not yet experts on change. They may know what the organization needs, but very little about what can be done or the kind of changes that are possible. That is why the first major learning activity of the Change Team is to learn about change.

Help the team take a broader, strategic view of the organization. Participants of the Change Team often have a narrow viewpoint of the organization and the change process. They will often focus their attention on their own functions' needs. Yet success of the overall change depends on the ability of the Change Team and the organization as a whole to take a system-wide, strategic view of the organization as a whole.

The kind of learning that is essential includes:

- Learning what other organizations have done to change (benchmarking, visiting organizations, participating in professional organizations and conferences)

- Training to identify and work through the key human changes that the team will need to manage

- Learning how to communicate change effectively

- Training on the dynamics of change

- Awareness about the importance of symbolic as well as tangible action

- Structuring collaborative planning and employee involvement

As they learn about change, the team will become both committed to the change, and capable of undertaking the process of planning and designing the change with the organization.

The Change Navigator, and other resource people (consultants and change leaders from other organizations) who are brought in, have a huge task. They have to create a graduate-level learning process about organizational change, on a just-in-time basis to get the Change Team up to speed. But short-changing this task will lead to more limited and less sophisticated change designs in the future. Educating the Change Team is an up-front investment that has a high pay-off. The members of the team in turn become coaches and teachers to key people throughout the organization in key change skills.

Create a Vision and Plan the Change Process

The Change Team has several tasks to get started:

- Refining and adding more specificity to the strategic vision set by the Leadership Team

- Looking at the organization's current state capability and the obstacles to change it must overcome

- Creating processes for communicating and engaging the whole organization in change

Refining Strategic Vision

From data regarding the need for change and the framework of the strategic vision from the leadership team, the Change Team must develop a clearer picture of where they want to go, including a specific image of what they want to develop. This is analogous to moving from a broad sense of what is needed, to beginning to create an architectural design. There are many references the team can draw on in creating the vision of the change. The vision should include:

- A picture of what the organization or business unit will look like after they change

- Key deliverables and milestones

- Measures of success

Defining Current State

Many organizations know where they want to go, but they aren't realistic or informed about the current reality, the obstacles that the organization faces in changing itself. The Change Team will sometimes have to gather information on the culture of the organization that the Leadership Team is not aware of. They must gather information on the level of skills that currently exist, how willing and able people are to change, and look at the previous history of the organization in changing itself.

Tasks 3 and 4 represent activities that the Change Team can undertake to gather information about the current state. In Task 3 they will conduct workshops to teach employees about the demands of change, which will also open up a channel of communication about current mindsets, concerns, and readiness to change. The assessment process of Task 4 will surface deeper and more comprehensive information on the previous experiences of change and how the organization is ready and able to change.

It is particularly important that the Change Team understand the sources of resistance and concerns of the employees, and the extent to which the proposed changes will run counter to the existing culture and style of the organization.

Engage the Broader Organization

Agree on how the team will gather input and ideas from the larger organization as they guide the change process. Ensure the team does not position itself in a way that invites resentment on the part of the organization—that it does not create a we/they or in-group/out-group dynamic.

The Change Team will be the initiator of many of the key activities in each stage of change. For example, they will initiate the processes to engage employees in developing change awareness and capability (Task 3). The process of design will involve other parts of the organization. This planning process has been called the "accordian" process because it contains coming-together points where the team works, and then moves out to share and gather feedback from the rest of the organization. If the rest of the organization is not aware of what the Change Team is doing at any point in time, then they are risking the future commitment and engagement of the rest of the organization.

The next step is to develop Individual Change Capability (see Task 3), and design a communication plan for sharing information with the organization and getting input from the organization.

TASK 3: DEVELOP INDIVIDUAL CHANGE CAPABILITY

Key Activities

■ *Develop Change Capability Workshop*

SETTING THE COURSE

Organizations frequently wait too long before they tell their employees about proposed changes; so most people find out through the grapevine. The leaders feel that if they tell people too soon they will lose productivity and divert attention from the task at hand. They make a grave mistake. First, people are already diverted by the uncertainty about what will happen. Second, they need time to prepare themselves for the changes and support to do that. And third, by not engaging the people in the organization they do not surface important information bearing on the organization's capability to change.

While the specific nature of some of the changes is not yet clear, the general skills and direction is clear, and the sooner people begin to prepare, the more ready they will be to change. So, the first wave of change cannot end until everyone in the organization is briefed about the change and helped to begin to prepare to take up the new roles.

Core Activities

Outcomes

- Conducting employee workshops to develop agility and the ability to thrive in the pressure of deep and continuous change

- Provide a process for all employees to develop the new workplace roles, skills, and mindsets that will help them succeed in the transformed workplace

- Employees who understand external changes as triggers for internal change

- Employees with the skills to function in the change process

- Employees who overcome denial and resistance, and are ready to commit to the demands of change

- Employees who are excited about the possibilities of the new workplace they can help create, and understand the need to adopt new roles and expectations

- Employees who make early input into the design of the change process, sharing their concerns, potential difficulties, and ideas about how to implement change

CHALLENGES

What Will It Mean to Me?

When change is initiated, it should be no surprise that the first response of employees is about their own future and how they can adapt to the change. Job security is the first concern, and until people know whether they have a future, and what they need to do to prepare for it, they will not be ready to help the organization succeed. By waiting to address these personal concerns, the organization keeps their people on hold, sacrificing time and productivity while people wait to see what will happen.

Of course, the exact nature of the change is still to be worked out. But employees can be brought into the process by letting them know the general direction of change and helping them to prepare themselves for a difficult task. Using an overall "map" is a good way to introduce the major components and direction.

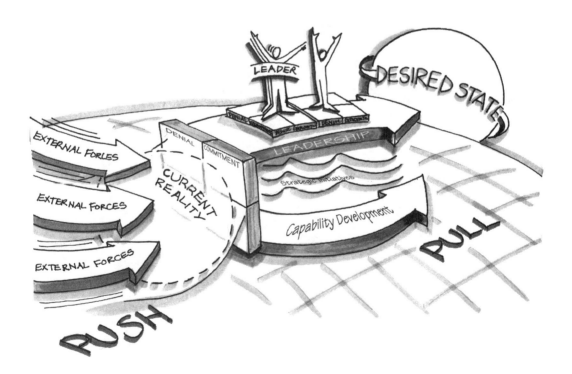

Just as the Change Team needed to learn about change, so employees need some education and preparation to be part of the change process. If they are treated as passive recipients, waiting to be told what to do, they will not be real partners in the success of the organization.

Change Demands New Skills, Mindsets and Ways of Seeing Work

Employees need more than commitment to succeed at change, they need help to understand the new expectations of the process-centered workplace, and how to assess their own ability and desire to work in new ways.

Reaction to change is often determined by fear of the unknown, lack of preparation for change and inadequate skills for managing change. People in an organization need to be prepared for change, because dealing with change isn't a natural skill.

The ability of people to change is increasingly a requirement for competitive advantage. The more effective people are at managing change, the more successful an organization will be. The only predictable future is that change will continue.

Current ways of thinking and working are deeply ingrained and heavily reinforced by existing systems and structures. It is the employees who have to make the change successful. But after a major change they often don't know how to do the job in a new way. They don't know how to make the decision about whether to leave or stay.

Tapping Energy for Change

Multiple organizational transitions can sap the trust and willingness of individuals to change. People can get worn down to change, and the planning of change initiatives has to take into account people's ability to absorb waves of change.

The core capabilities of personal change management in individuals are often underdeveloped. Individual change mastery has often been thought of as a discretionary or "soft" skill, and therefore has often been left out of the planning and implementation process. In fact, it is the critical skill for creating effective change.

Leadership often does not experience the level of discomfort and chaos that employees do, and therefore gaps of perception often arise. Leaders either have had more time to prepare for change, or have more information about why change has to happen. They often aren't aware that the rest of the organization needs this same information in order to become comfortable with change.

Employees Need to Share Responsibility for Change

Employees feel that change isn't their problem; change is only the responsibility of top leaders or a special group. If people act like the leaders will take care of them, they will not take the responsibility, initiative, or develop real commitment to self-development during the change process.

Employees tend to focus narrowly on their special area, which limits their ability to see the overall need and direction for change. When there is a major change effort, every employee has to develop a broader, more strategic big-picture view of the organization.

GUIDING PRINCIPLES

■ *Engage the human factors, the emotional side of change.* Change is upsetting, disorienting, and difficult. People need explicit support and help to move through their denial and resistance to change before they can become a meaningful part of a change initiative. Be willing to invest resources to support employees through the change process.

■ *The quicker this process is initiated, the quicker the change can take place.* Changing attitudes, engaging people, and building the new workplace take a considerable amount of time. The earlier you address these issues, the quicker you will be able to implement change and obtain the desired results. It is never too early to begin to engage the workforce in the needed changes.

■ *The use of repeatable models and common language will help all members of the organization discuss and address change.* Putting everyone through the same program enables all employees, managers, and stakeholders to speak about the change in the same terms, provides them with a shared experience they can fall back on, and provides a framework for holding discussions and addressing concerns.

■ *Leaders need to be visible at the earliest phases of change.* Employees are used to seeing what the leaders do, and what they reward, especially if they conflict with what is said. Employees need training and reinforcement in new ways to work, and the organizational reward and management systems have to work differently in order to get employees to behave differently.

■ *Honesty and candor build trust.* People will see through unrealistic forecasts, contradictory statements, and visions that do not reflect what is possible. These will only serve to damage credibility and will hinder the development of a coalition for change. Honesty, even if difficult, will allow a shared basis of respect on which dialogue can be built.

■ *Create several successive change awareness events throughout the organization before implementing change.* Commitment to change is a process that moves through several phases and activities, and involves many people. Several successive change events throughout the organization, from top to bottom, are necessary to build commitment, and a realistic understanding of the change process and what it will demand.

■ *Since new possibilities propel change, the new organization should challenge conventional and prevailing wisdom.* Change is better and faster when employees are excited about what their organization can be, not just what it has to do.

■ *You need to change both mindsets and behavior in employees to get them to make a change achieve its potential.* Individuals need to develop a new set of thoughts (mindsets) about work and the sets of skills and capabilities to put these thoughts into action. Recruitment, orientation, and performance management processes must be adjusted to emphasize the new skills and mindsets. It is difficult to help people shift their mindset until you demonstrate how and why their tasks are shifting. Experientially based learning is the fastest way to acquire this learning. The process should allow people to explore and question the new mindsets. The acquisition of new skills is developmental and will require reinforcement through application. Shifting identity anchors is a part of learning these new skills.

KEY ACTIVITIES FOR TASK 3

ACTIVITY 1: Develop Change Capability Workshop

Create a one- or two-day, large-group workshop offered to large (40–200-person) groups to introduce information on change and organizational design possibilities that can set up an inquiry/exploration process in a cross-section of the organization. This workshop helps to prepare the whole organization to recognize the critical path for the future and gather the skills as individuals to make the change.

The workshops can be offered in many different work settings, for diverse and varied groups of employees. The workshop will convene one large or several smaller, cross-functional workshops to:

- Explore the current changes in the work environment, customer experiences and needs

- Explore the context in which the organization must operate

- Develop a sense of the possible forms that the redesigned organization can take

- Create the mindset to expect major changes

The workshop will respond first to the personal side of change. They are designed to develop emotional literacy—the ability to be sensitive to the real impacts of change, both mental and emotional, by exploring the human factors involved in the implementation process:

- Past experiences with change implementation

- Emotional responses of different groups to change

- Principles used to work the change process

- Underlying concerns

- Current culture's acceptance of the change

- Level of employee involvement

The workshop will also initiate the two-way communication process between the Leadership and Change Team, and the rest of the organization. The message about the need for change and the seriousness of the commitment, will be personally delivered by leaders. A channel for communication from employees will be set up, and the Change Team will be introduced.

It can be offered at different times to different groups, and cascaded down through the organization as the design process begins. It should be used to open up people to possibilities prior to their becoming engaged in the design or implementation process. The workshop, or elements of it, will be cascaded through the organization as follows:

- Leadership Team: as part of their alignment process (Task 1)

- Change Team: prior to their beginning the vision process (Task 2)

- Cross-sectional groups within the organization: before they are given actual designs to implement or respond to proposals

NAVIGATION TOOL:
CHANGE CAPABILITY WORKSHOP

A 1–2 day learning experience to:

- Prepare people to understand and accept change

- Create skills to work effectively in the new workplace

- Develop new skills and mindsets

TEMPLATE OF WORKSHOP PROCESS

Introduction

The organizational leader or a key member of the Change Team convenes the sessions. The convener frames the session as having three purposes:

- To fully explain the purpose and outline of a proposed change

- To elicit concerns, responses and ideas from the affected group

- To design a process for ongoing involvement in the coming change

Picture of Change

This helps participants get into emotional responses to change, and offers a non-threatening way for people to begin to talk about upsetting and difficult reactions and concerns about change. The facilitator should not probe too deeply and strive for any consensus, just help people feel comfortable talking to each other, and perhaps open up some feelings issues.

Each person is asked to take a large piece of paper and some colored markers, and draw a picture of their experience of change. The picture should communicate their feelings about the changes that are happening in the organization, in a way that should have meaning to a person who does not speak English (e.g., there should be no written words).

After a few minutes, people compare their pictures at table groups, or if there are no more than 20 participants, with the whole group. Answer the following questions in the discussion:

- What are the differences?

- What are the similarities?

- What feelings, concerns and issues are common to the pictures?

The tables then each share the highlights of their discussion with the whole group. The leader records their key images and themes on a large piece of paper or two flip charts side-by-side, and then asks the group to draw linkages between the areas.

Hopes and Fears

Each person is invited to share very briefly a word that summarizes their hopes about change. Then people go around again and share a word communicating their fears about change.

Presentation about Change Initiative

The leader, or Change Team member, presents an overview of the proposed change, why it is being undertaken, and the process by which change will be designed and implemented, as it exists at this early stage.

The leader gives a 10–20 minute presentation on why the organization is going through the change process. The presentation should include:

- What it is that is going on in the business environment that is leading the organization to go through the change

- What are the *internal* factors driving the organization to change

- What organizational outcomes are needed from the proposed change process

- What the implications are if nothing is implemented, or if the change effort is unsuccessful

While some of what is said will be known, it is important for the leader to candidly present the dilemma the organization faces and to solicit questions and responses.

The leader communicates his or her expectations of the change initiative, including:

- Specific change expectations and parameters

- Expectations on how this group is impacted or affected by the change

- Specific timeline on when he or she expects the work to be done

- Resources available

Video (optional)

The presentation would be greatly enhanced if it included a video of the CEO or leader of the business unit making the case for change. The video could include other elements, such as input from customers, interviews with members of the Change Team, and some information on the need to change and the proposed scope of the change.

A copy of the video or presentation material on the change should be available for participants to bring back to their groups after the workshop.

Response to the Change Initiative Presentation

The resulting exchange builds commitment, trust and understanding between the leadership and the stakeholder group. It begins the process of having leaders listen, and stakeholders share their responses.

The participants should meet at their tables, answering the questions:

- What did we hear?
- What needs further clarification?
- What concerns us?
- What "burning questions" do we have?

Each table group (or the whole group if less than twenty) should share their answers on flip charts. Leaders respond after all tables or everyone has presented.

The leader invites input and questions from the group who offer their input, ideas, concerns and questions. The facilitator invites dialogue.

Why It is Hard to Change

Ask about some of the ways that organizations, groups and people resist change. Ask what are some of the good reasons that they resist change. Get some of their comments.

Present some of the leading reasons people resist change, referring to their suggestions as you do this:

- They aren't informed

- They aren't involved in the process

- They fear they will lose control

- They don't know whether they have the new skills

- They will lose what is comfortable and familiar and easy for them

- They will lose power

Your Response to Change

One of the biggest factors that will determine how you move through this change will be how you have experienced changes in the past. Have participants think about a change they have experienced in the past. Ask them to recall what it was like for them at the beginning of the change. Imagine that they had kept a diary, what would they have recorded about their thoughts, feelings and experiences?

> *Flip through the pages to the time where you became convinced that a change was happening. It was real, and you were going to be affected. Recall your thoughts, feelings and actions. Remember what you said to*

yourself. Now flip ahead to where the change was about 52 percent done—over halfway. At that point, what were your thoughts, feelings and actions? Finally, think about the time when the change seemed pretty much complete. What were your thoughts, feelings and actions?

Peoples responses to this exercise formed the basis of a model that helps describe and frame responses during change.

Model of Transition Curve

People go through four phases in coming to accept a change. These phases are normal and predictable. During each phase an individual does important work that will help them accept the change. The phases progress, one after another, with each stage building on the work of the prior stage. Although most people will work through all four stages, they move through at different speeds. Individuals, groups and organizations can become stuck in any stage.

Moving through change represents a shift from seeing change as a danger or threat, to seeing it as an opportunity. At first we almost inevitably see a change, especially one we do not initiate ourselves, as a danger.

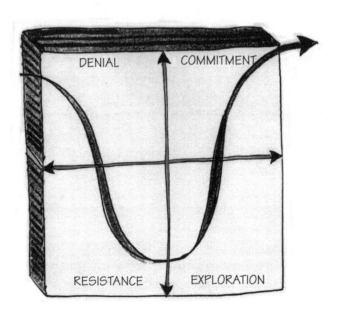

PHASE ONE: Denial. The first phase of change is called denial. It begins when you first become aware that change is on the horizon. It is hard to spot denial in yourself because it is an inner attempt to minimize, dismiss and protect yourself from the disruption of change. On the surface, people appear calm and rational. Denial often masks inner turmoil.

If denial is so quiet on the surface, how can you recognize denial in yourself and others? One way is to see how much time people spend talking about the change. If some people are acting like nothing is going on, while other are discussing the change, the first group is in denial. If a group refuses to talk about or plan for the change, they are in denial. People in denial:

- Avoid the topic

- Appear unconcerned

- Refuse to take initiative

- Act like nothing is happening

- Only do routine work

Denial is normal and predictable. Frequently, denial is helpful. It may keep people from worrying unnecessarily, or from taking attention off their normal work before there is any real information available about how the change will affect them. However, denial can be destructive if people continue to ignore signs that they need to begin to do things differently.

One way you can test yourself for denial is to see if you are more closed than normal to outside information. Are you ignoring sources of company information that you usually pay attention to? Do you find yourself irritated and unwilling to engage in conversation with people you normally look to for information? One way to move yourself through denial is to ask questions about what is going on and how other people are experiencing change.

PHASE TWO: Resistance. The second phase of change is resistance. Resistance begins when people can no longer deny the change or ignore their reactions to the change. However, they have still not accepted that they have to cooperate with the change. Resistance begins when people begin to let reality sink in—and want to fight against letting the change happen.

People can resist change in several ways. There is passive resistance, when people just quietly go on with business as usual, in spite of instructions to begin doing things differently. Then there is active resistance, with people loudly trying to argue why the change is a bad idea, or why they should not be required to change.

Resistance can be very uncomfortable. You may be uncomfortable because you are confused between the old way and the new way. You may feel insecure, not sure what you are supposed to do, how you are supposed to do it, or how you will be evaluated. You may not be very confident as you begin to think about doing things in a new way.

People in resistance:

- Show anger at the company

- Complain

- Become passive

- Act exhausted and overwhelmed

How can you listen to people's resistance to learn what you aware not are of? People in resistance say things like:

- "Why me?"

- "They can't make me change."

- "This will never work."

- "What a dumb idea."

As a leader it is important to distinguish "loyal" resistance, where people are negative because they are pointing up real difficulties with the change or plan that have not been anticipated, from the negativity of initial resistance.

Resistance, too, is normal and predictable. Resistance gives people time to learn that they can be successful in the new way. Active resistance can serve to surface issues that need to be resolved before the change can be successfully implemented. However, once these issues have been surfaced and addressed, people need to move on.

PHASE THREE: Exploration. After resistance, people move into exploration. People move into exploration after acknowledging and accepting that the change is necessary or required. At this point, people begin to look at what is possible, to make the best of the change. You may experience a feeling of chaos or lack of focus as you try out new skills and approaches. You may have lots of energy one day, and the next feel overwhelmed by all the new things you need to learn.

People in exploration:

- Experiment

- Seek new ways

- Begin to create a vision of the possibilities of the future

- Take risks

- Generate lots of ideas

- Have trouble staying focused

People in exploration say things like:

- "This isn't so bad."

- "This could work."

- "Let me see what I can do about this."

- "I have some ideas."

Exploration gives people time to experiment and try out new ways of doing things. People begin to discover how to make the change work for them. It provides a time to plan, to learn, and to form a new picture of the future. During exploration, try to resist deciding on the first idea or possible action.

PHASE FOUR: Commitment. The fourth stage of change is commitment. People have experimented and settled on an approach that will work for them, have become more comfortable with the new ways and assume responsibility for making the change work. They also feel a sense of accomplishment and increased self confidence.

Commitment comes when you have learned new ways to go forward. You understand why you have gone through the change. You experience pride and accomplishment that you have effectively completed the process of change. At this point, it is important to reward yourself for success.

People in commitment:

- Feel in control

- Feel comfortable

- Take time to affirm and recognize their efforts

- Reflect on what they have learned

- Start looking ahead to the next change

People in commitment say things like:

- "I can't remember how we used to do this."

- "I think our new way of working is better."

- "I wonder what will change next."

Commitment is the reward for going through the changes. Acknowledge and reward yourself. Take note of the things that helped you get through this change successfully. Think about how you could build on these lessons the next time you need to change. Don't let yourself get too comfortable, because the next change is coming soon. Keep informed so you won't deny the next change.

Becoming Part of the Change

To assist people in moving through change ask participants to apply these stages to the change process in their organization.

Now ask them specifically what do they feel would make it more or less difficult for them to be part of the coming changes.

Write up on a flip chart a + and –, and list various factors. When the list is complete, vote on the pros and cons, put numbers on the list so that everyone can see the priority order.

The group will end up with a list of factors that they need more of and less of, in order for them to be a part of the change process.

The Change Team member or leader might offer some guidance about how these factors can be facilitated or minimized.

The group should then be encouraged to brainstorm in table groups. Each group should take one of the top pros and top cons and brainstorm how they can overcome them, and what support would be essential, useful and good to have.

Post a list of factors in some visible place in the organization and update it with the list of factors from each succeeding workshop.

Methods for Focusing Action

Post some of the important issues that they feel the organization needs to address in order to really succeed at change. Then they rank them from most to least important. Then they go around the room, with each person sharing their most important issue the organization needs to address.

When the key issues up front are in clusters, give people two colors of adhesive dots:

- They will have five dots of each color

- One color refers to issues that their own group has direct influence over

- The other color refers to the most important issues for the organization to address

- Participants go up to the board and place their colored dots on the five issues they feel their group has most control over, and the five most important issues

The group then lists the most important issues and those the group has most control over.

Strategy for Addressing Issues

Depending on the size of the group, either groups at different tables can take the most important issues or the whole group can address them together.

For the most important issues, develop a set of suggested strategies for how the organization or the Change Team could work on the issue.

Next, tackle the issues their group has influence or control over. For each one, they should brainstorm ways to get involved and define a strategy for using their influence.

Balancing Involvement with Action

Point out that participating in planning a large change is a delicate task. On the one hand, some small group needs to take responsibility and do it. On the other, there needs to be broad input and involvement.

Ask them to consider how they want to be part of the change process.

Elicit specific suggestions focused on:

- What they want from the Change Team

- What they want to be able to do, or how they want to be part of the process

- How they as a group or as individuals, can prepare themselves for change

Questions about the Change

What do we still need to know about the change? Make a list of questions, find out who is responsible, and when there will be an answer.

Next Steps and Further Activities

Make plans for a next step or follow-up to this session.

As an outcome of the workshop the facilitator/Change Team member must:

- Follow up with answers to questions

- Send complete notes of all information about workshops to participants within one month of the last workshop

The next step is to assess organizational change capability, as detailed in Task 4.

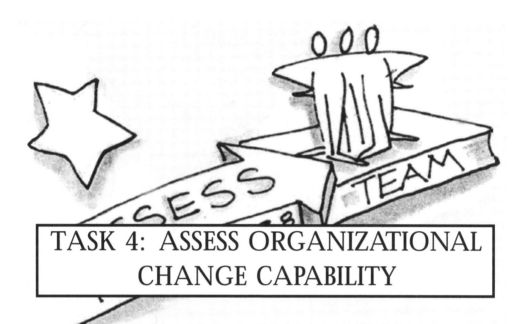

TASK 4: ASSESS ORGANIZATIONAL CHANGE CAPABILITY

Key Activities

■ *Convene and Charter Assessment Team*

■ *Design and Set Up Assessment Process*

■ *Data Collection*

■ *Feedback and Action Steps*

SETTING THE COURSE

Change does not begin with a blank slate in the organization. The history of the organization, its previous experience with change, and its culture and values, will all determine how it goes about changing. This task involves exploring the organization's current capability for change. Using interviews, surveys and focus groups, the Change Navigator will help the organization determine the internal strengths as well as the obstacles to change.

The Organizational Change Capability Assessment process provides a focused inquiry into many dimensions of an organization and its people. It is conducted by the Change Navigator who partners with the Change Team or an Assessment Team within the organization.

The assessment explores how each part of the organization defines, acts on, and responds to change. Its purpose is to define and focus the attention of the organization on:

- Internal challenges faced in implementing change

- Areas to leverage its change efforts

The process helps the organization be proactive about their change planning by anticipating difficulties and obstacles, and practicing preventive intervention.

The systematic assessment process brings the organization information about itself that it does not know. Often, the common ways that the organization resists or responds to change are not obvious to the people in the organization. These organizational blind spots then get in the way of establishing an effective change initiative.

In addition, the initial assessment offers an opportunity for the Change Leaders to get to know the organization deeply and thoroughly, and begin the process of working in partnership with the people in the organization to facilitate effective change.

Core Activities

Outcomes

■ Identify and share understanding of the culture of the whole organization, as well as employees' concerns, resistances, and opportunities to leverage change throughout the organization

■ Assess organizational change capability through interviews, focus groups, and surveys, and share findings with the organization

■ Bring the data to the key Change Leaders to inform their planning of the process of change

■ People across the organization share their perceptions of the organization's strengths and weaknesses

■ Leaders obtain clear and detailed information about the organization's readiness and capacity to succeed in major change initiatives

■ The whole organization develops a clear picture of the issues, resistance, and opportunities inherent in the change process

■ Leaders, managers, and employees understand the gaps between the way things are and the way the must be in order to sustain real change

CHALLENGES

Top Leadership Isolated from Organizational Issues

The people who are in charge of a change often have an overly rosy view of how easy it will be, and may not be fully aware of the internal difficulties they have to overcome. Leaders are impatient to get on with change and they can be out of touch with the difficulties that change presents to the people in the organization. The cost of this denial will be difficulties in implementing a change, and unexpected reactions by the organization to their initiatives.

Change Sponsors may make unrealistic assessments of morale, ability to change and internal difficulties. People concerned with change don't want to hear about difficulties, or they don't understand the reasons that people would feel differently about it. They need clear, unfiltered information to plan realistically.

Resistance Blamed on Individuals Must be Understood

Resistance to change often arises from elements of the culture, such as special interests, narrow focus of attention by specialized functional groups and the effects of previous attempts at change. Resistance is natural and inevitable in an organization. It is not due to lack of motivation, but represents the reasonable responses of employees. Resistance and its sources must be uncovered, understood and responded to, or they can ruin a well planned change initiative.

Past Change Failures Affect the Current Initiative

Skepticism from previous initiatives and incomplete change efforts can make employees unwilling to commit to new change. Unless it makes a major effort to resolve them, past mistakes and resistance to change will be repeated in the present effort, largely because the organization is not aware of them. People need to be prepared for a different type of change initiative.

GUIDING PRINCIPLES

■ ***Organizations need to know where they are in order to decide what they have to change.*** This assessment can be considered a way to sense the organization's "temperature," its capability and orientation toward achieving success at change, and the potential pitfalls and challenges it faces along the way.

The assessment process is first conducted early in the change process, so that the organization and the people who lead the change can anticipate and respond to actual and potential obstacles to effective and sustainable change. It can be repeated at regular intervals to look objectively at progress and areas that need continuing attention.

By surfacing "hard" as well as "soft" data, it is possible to get the organization to see their challenges and obstacles to change more clearly. This process helps the organization become aware of its sometimes not obvious, even hidden, expectations, attitudes, and expectations related to change.

■ ***Cultural barriers to change should be identified and addressed early in the change process.*** The earlier they are addressed, the more chance there is of getting to the real cause of issues and of being able to move obstacles or design around them. The up-front costs of anticipating a difficulty is always less than dealing with it later on, and it is easier to be proactive than to exercise damage control later.

■ ***Information about the inner state of the organization must be gathered from many sources.*** You cannot start real change without a realistic picture of the internal climate of the organization. The assessment offers an objective and comprehensive picture to the people in the organization who "think they know it all."

The assessment utilizes three different sources of information:

1. **Interviews** with key people through the organization, and face-to-face discussions with the Leadership Team and a selection of other key leaders across the organization. They provide a confidential opportunity for a key individual to go into depth about the organization and the particular issues it faces in initiating change. They are useful to identify key issues and challenges, and to interpret findings from surveys.

2. **Focus groups** representing a cross-section of the groups that will be affected are small group discussions with 7–12 members of key functions and teams. They provide both broad and indepth information about people's way of seeing change. They offer an opportunity for people to share their views in depth about a proposed change, and how the organization works in general.

3. **Surveys** of employee perceptions of the organization's capabilities from a confidential questionnaire sent to all employees, provides broad information from the whole organization—a snapshot of how many people in an organization feel about particular issues at one point in time.

Each data source offers an important, but incomplete, perspective on the organization's readiness for a major change initiative. Together, the three methods provide a comprehensive picture of the readiness of the organization to change, and the challenges and difficulties it will face in achieving the results of change.

■ *Encourage upward pressure for change by making the top leadership aware of what the people below think, feel, do, and want to do.* The pressure from upward information can be critical. Leaders may need help, in the form of a push and some information from lower in the organization, before they can do what is needed to create real change. The people below the leadership often know more about what is needed, the real problems and the potential solutions, than their bosses.

■ *Plans need to be made to overcome resistance.* Resistance to change is natural and inevitable. Plans need to be made to overcome it. This begins with obtaining a realistic picture of the internal sources of resistance, why they exist, and taking them seriously.

KEY ACTIVITIES FOR TASK 4

ACTIVITY 1: Convene and Charter Assessment Team

The assessment is one of the first tasks of the change process. It forms the cornerstone for the change leadership activities of a change initiative. It should begin as soon as possible and be completed within several weeks. It can possibly be repeated during or after implementation.

The assessment process has two goals:

- Develop information that the organization trusts

- Build a collaborative problem-solving relationship with the client

Full or preliminary results of the assessment will be presented at various change-planning and design workshops, to help leaders, individuals, and the Change Team prepare for the change process.

To accomplish this, the entire assessment process must be conducted by an Assessment Team. The 4–6 person Assessment Team, convened by the leadership, contains:

- Key leaders from operational groups affected by the change

- Representatives of the different levels of the organization who are asked to provide information

- Human resources or organizational development people who conduct employee surveys and assessments

The task of the team is to define, communicate, gather, and use information about the organization. This may be their first opportunity to work together with the Leadership Team to set direction, guidelines, and projected outcomes for the assessment process, and to determine what they need to know about the organization and change.

Announce the initiation of the assessment process to the organization, with information on who will be included and how it will be done.

ACTIVITY 2: Design and Set Up Assessment Process

Construct an interview, focus group, and survey-based assessment process, with data collected from the groups who are involved in or affected by the broad change processes taking place in the organization.

The assessment gathers information from several levels of the organization: leadership, team, individual, and organizational, and asks respondents to describe the way things are, and the way they feel the organization should be in order to be effective at mastering change.

The Change Navigator and Assessment Team arrange to conduct interviews with key leaders and representatives of other groups critical to the change, focus groups for various employee groups who will be affected, and if possible a full organization survey.

Assessment Team Defines Focus Areas for Interviews and Focus Groups.
Determine what Change Leaders need to know about the organization and change:

- How fully is the organization aware of itself (i.e., does what it says about itself, and what the leadership says, fit with actuality)?

- How deep are the internal challenges to the proposed change process?

Select key questions the organization wants to explore through assessment. The focus is on how people experience change in the organization, what has worked and what has not, and on how the organization deals with change. Other questions should be about how the individual or group interviewed sees the need for change, and how the organization allows people and groups to suggest changes and new ways. The process can ask people and groups about elements of the organization that people experience as possible obstacles to success at change.

Decide the format of interviews and focus groups. Design the logistics of the process. Select people to interview and set up a process to ask for volunteers who will be asked to join focus groups in key areas of the organization.

Inform the organization about purpose, outcomes, and expectations of the assessment. Announce the assessment to the organization through a variety of channels.

Assessment Team Customizes Survey Instrument, and Defines Logistics and Timeline. Customize the survey, drawing questions from the Change Navigation Tool and other sources, using language that will be relevant and familiar to the respondents. Revise or rework questions to fit the current needs, change history and culture of the organization. Consider other questions that might be important, and other areas that should be added to the survey. Focus on fewer, rather than more questions.

The design survey introduction where the respondent is asked to respond either to past history or responding to change, specific past changes or the current wave of changes, should be written to reflect exactly what changes the respondent should consider in answering the questions.

Outline each activity of the survey process, with timelines, who is responsible, and how they will be done. Define how the data will be reported back to the company, including the different divisions, business units or work groups who will receive feedback reports.

The Assessment Team, Change Team and top leadership announce the assessment process, its purpose, how it will be conducted, how and when results will be reported, and the expected outcomes.

It is critical that employees:

- Know about the assessment process

- Understand why it is being done

- Believe that it will not be the basis for any performance evaluation

- Expect to see the results themselves in summary form

Set up a series of face-to-face information meetings about the assessment process. Key managers and division leaders should be briefed in person so that they will not be overly concerned about the evaluative potential of the survey. Designate a contact person for further information.

Activity 3: Data Collection

Conduct interviews, focus groups and surveys. It is usually best to begin with the interviews, then design the survey and begin the focus groups. Focus groups can be held after the survey is done, to help to further understand and focus on some of the key issues defined in the interviews and survey data.

The purpose is to develop a picture of the current culture of the organization, how it works, what it expects from employees, how it sees change and elements that resist changing.

Conduct Interviews and Focus Groups

The interview and focus groups should target the key areas outlined in the Change Navigation Tool above. Asking an individual or focus group to talk about these factors will usually lead to a great deal of information.

Interview key stakeholders and leaders about the change. Conduct focus groups throughout the organization.

It is important to preserve the confidentiality of the people who participate. The interviewer should record major themes and issues without identifying the individual.

Gather and transcribe all the information, and meet with a team of people to explore key issues and analyze the results. Look for common themes and how extensive they are.

Distribute Surveys to the Organization

This survey is offered anonymously to:

- Every employee or the parts of the organization initiating major change

- A cross-section of employees of the whole organization

Its purpose is to help the whole organization get a picture of where they are in relation to change in general, or in relation to a specific change. It allows comparisons between internal groups and other organizations in a database.

Notices are sent out after about a week, reminding people to respond. Extra assessments are made available for people who misplaced theirs. Employees should know they can obtain further information about the survey by contacting members of the Assessment Team.

NAVIGATION TOOL:
AREAS OF FOCUS FOR ASSESSMENT PROCESS

The interviews and the focus groups can be conducted in a semi-structured process, allowing people to move through at their own pace. The interviews, focus groups, and surveys explore key factors that have been found to directly affect the organization's change capacity. The interviewer or focus group leader should introduce each topic, then ask several questions to focus the person or group's responses in that area:

- **Leadership Engagement**
  How leaders actively help employees understand and accept that change is part of everything they do, and integrate it into their strategic and operational action.

- **Communication and Involvement**
  How the organization is kept informed; how all people are part of designing and implementing change.

- **Empowerment**
  How employees are willing to take action and risks, and to say and do what is needed to support effective change.

- **Learning and Innovation**
  How the whole organization is open to learning, trying new ways and initiating innovative actions.

- **Teamwork**
  How people collaborate in teams, across boundaries and within their functional area, to focus on the broad mission and vision.

- **Value People**
  How leaders and employees value, respect, support and help people deal with the stress of change.

- **Aligned Policies and Work Processes**
  How the organization supports and reinforces its values and new ways through infrastructure, policies, values and practices.

The facilitator should introduce each topic and help each member of the group contribute ideas. The facilitator should also try to help people amplify and follow up each others comments. The challenge is to guide the group along from topic to topic, but not to inhibit the exchange, and to get below the surface to get the best information. Make sure that everyone speaks and try to limit any individual's amount of air time. Paraphrase issues you hear, and ask if your statement is correct. A recorder should record notes from what is said on a computer.

Guidelines for Interviews and Focus Groups

While there are certain important differences between interviewing an individual and a group, there are some major guidelines for setting up and conducting interviews and focus groups:

- **Inform the Organization about the Process Before You Begin**
  Inform not just the people who will be interviewed, but the colleagues of those you interview, and indeed the whole organization, about the purposes and activities of the assessment process. Create a written explanation, and hold one or more informational meetings.

  If you do not build trust and confidence in the fairness, integrity, and confidentiality of the assessment at the beginning, you will have to face distrust, resentment, and lack of cooperation in the data gathering, which in turn leads to poor information and lack of willingness of the organization to follow through.

- **Keep Agreements and Follow Up the Process**
  Since the assessment takes place at an early phase of the process, it is critical to the overall success of change that the Assessment Team model openness by making sure that the organization, especially the individuals who are interviewed and part of focus groups, receive feedback in a timely manner and get a chance to respond to the findings.

- **Make the Process Clear from the Start**
  When you recruit or first make contact with a prospective person, make it very clear:

  —What you are doing
  —Why you are doing it
  —How you are doing it
  —What the person who offers information will receive in return

- **Tell How the Data Will Be Used**
  People will be more willing to trust and have a better idea of what to talk about, if they understand how the data will be used and the purpose of the assessment.

- **Offer Safeguards for Confidentiality**
  Tell the person how confidentiality will be assured:

  —Names will not be linked with the information they give (e.g., people in focus group will not have to say their name)

  —When they give examples or share concerns, no names of people or work groups will be solicited

  —While data will be recorded from interviews and focus groups, no names will be linked with particular statements

  —Statements which might identify a particular person will be deleted

  —Results will only contain general concerns and issues, no reference to particular groups or names of people

  —No reports will be offered on particular people, and the management will not be given confidential assessments of people or problems

- **Offer Opportunity to See Final Report and Respond to It**
  Let people know they will receive a copy of the final report and when they can expect it. Offer a way to make input and respond to the final report, either by calling the interviewer, by responding by e-mail or voice mail, or writing to the Assessment, Design, or Leadership Team. Offer individuals and focus groups copies of the transcripts of their interviews for their reference.

Guidelines for Holding Interviews

Setting Up Interviews

Call people you want to interview and set up appointments. Refer to the informational meeting that they attended about the assessment process. Repeat on the phone a brief explanation of the purposes of the interview. Let them know that you want to spend some time with each individual talking about their perceptions of the organization's readiness to lead change.

Stress that the interviews will be confidential, that information will not be connected with any individual, and that you will not ask for individual names in the interview. They need to know that you will not share what they say with their boss, and that what they say has nothing to do with evaluating their own competence to manage change.

Ask to schedule a period of time where they can talk candidly and where you will not be interrupted. Arrange for one uninterrupted hour.

Schedule all the interviews as quickly as you can, and do it soon after you have presented your purposes to the organization or Leadership Team. Paranoia can build very quickly if you wait too long, and people can forget why you are doing it. As busy as everyone is, strive to make appointments within a few days.

When possible, come to their offices or schedule a private meeting room. This helps you understand their environment and that of the organization.

Starting the Interview

Be on time. Share the ground rules and expectations before you begin. Make the confidentiality clear. State that you will be reporting your overall findings with its implications to the leadership group. Let them know that they will receive feedback and in what form. Begin the interview by asking them to talk about what they do and to give you a brief history of their career with the company.

Recording

The best way to gather data in interviews is with a portable computer. Notes are difficult to read and you cannot get enough down. Write as much as you can without feeling you have to take down every word.

Be sure to look up at the person regularly and maintain as much eye contact as you can. It is helpful to send a copy of your transcript and cleaned up notes to the person you interview for their records.

Posing Questions

Ask each question in general terms, trying to be open-ended, and not framing questions that have brief or Yes or No answers. When a person pauses, wait quietly to encourage them to continue. Ask many follow-up questions to make sure that you get their meaning. Keep asking for more information, and especially ask if they can give you an example of what they mean. From time to time you might repeat back what you understand of what they said, to see if you are understanding their point.

For example, when a person talks about something they learned or feel in general about the organization, ask them to give an example of what they mean, or to recall a time when that was true. The more specific details you get, the clearer your information will be.

While you can follow the individual themes in the interview, you should expect that the person will wander into related topics. Go with the flow of the interview, and then at the end you can go back and make sure you have hit every area.

Ending the Interview

Ask if they have anything more that they feel is important. Let them know when they can expect a copy of their remarks and when they can expect feedback. Remember, keep your word to them—your credibility is one of your most important assets as a consultant. Thank them for their participation and let them know how they can contact you if they have any questions or concerns.

NAVIGATION TOOL:
CONDUCTING INTERVIEWS AND FOCUS GROUPS

Why Do Interviews?

An intensive interview is a 1–2 hour, face-to-face, confidential conversation with a key person in the organization to gather their private perceptions and observations relating to organizational change.

There are two reasons for an interview: to get information, and to build support and commitment to change. Interviews thus gather information and build relationship. Both information and relationship are necessary to an effective change initiative:

- You want people's views and experience of the organization

- The interview can probe their resistance or difficulties with the change process, and through your exchange, you can perhaps help move them toward becoming committed to the change process

Whom to Interview

The Assessment Team should interview from 12–25 people, representing different levels, functions, and perspectives on the proposed change Begin with the top leaders and a cross-section of key people throughout the organization. Time constraints and the sense of how much you are learning in each interview, should guide your selections.

Interview beyond the formal group leaders. The more diverse the opinions of the groups, the more useful the information will be.

Select people who:

- Tend to be opinion leaders who are known for their perceptiveness, candor, and helpfulness

- Have been involved in previous or current change initiatives

This helps to gather the organization's experience in managing change.

Focus Groups

A focus group brings together 7–12 people, usually with a common work experience or role, to talk about their perceptions and ideas about change. They should sit around a table.

People should be clear about the purpose of the focus group and the safeguards on confidentiality, before they sign up. Nobody should come to a focus group except volunteers. Ask at the start, and excuse anyone who has not voluntarily chosen to come.

Make it clear that people do not have to identify themselves when they speak, and that they not use names when talking about issues or incidents.

NAVIGATION TOOL:
ORGANIZATIONAL CHANGE CAPABILITY SURVEY

There is no canned organizational survey that can fit the exact type of change that you are engaged in. Therefore, while you can utilize prepared surveys, the best way to create an organizational survey is to customize questions to fit your situation. The following statements have been developed by Changeworks, and seem to generally fit the major issues we see in achieving major change. A survey should probably not be more than 50–100 questions, so Assessment Teams should select from the following themes and questions to design their surveys.

The questions below follow the model of key areas in organizational culture that researchers have found to be important to change initiatives.

You may want to engage a consultant with experience in administering surveys to help you in the process of designing, implementing and analyzing results, if you want to survey more than a small group.

The traditional way to set up a survey is to ask people to respond to each question in the way they see their team, division or whole organization acting in relation to each questions on a 1–5 point scale, from most to least, or highly agree to highly disagree. Instructions should be carefully worded.

Sample Instructions

Think of the way that the managers (or top leaders or employees, depending on the question) of your organization and/or business unit have initiated or responded to recent changes. For each question, answer how much you agree or disagree with each question in relation to your perception of the top management of your organization, division or business unit.

SAMPLE SURVEY

LEADERSHIP ENGAGEMENT

Change Orientation

Leaders really want to see the organization succeed at change.

Leaders follow up change initiatives.

Leaders make their support of change clear and explicit.

Leaders inspire employees to support proposed changes.

Leaders are serious about implementing the changes they propose.

Leaders are not afraid of change.

Leaders do what is needed to make sure change succeeds.

Credibility

Leaders act in line with the organization's stated values and expectations.

Leaders tend to achieve what they say they will.

Leaders consider the whole organization, not just their own unit or specialty.

Leaders are competent to lead this organization.

Leaders tell the truth about changes.

Leaders can be trusted.

Leaders hold values that are consistent despite the change.

Leaders live their values.

Strategic Focus

Leaders are clear about the mission; what they are trying to achieve as a business.

Leaders have clear plans for short-term objectives and goals based on the mission and vision.

Leaders have a clear direction for the long-term future, based on the mission and vision.

Leaders' actions and decisions are connected to business outcomes.

Leaders focus on customer needs when they make decisions and allocate work.

Leaders act consistently and in alignment with each other.

Leaders achieve alignment between strategy, goals and resources.

Leaders maintain their focus, and do not get distracted during change.

Leaders relate changes to the organization's vision and mission.

Leaders help people understand how their work relates to other jobs, and to the organization's goals.

Recent changes have been helpful to the organization.

Leaders propose the changes that are really needed.

Leaders clearly prioritize changes, so they know what is important to achieve.
Leaders focus on the most important changes at one time, to avoid diluting resources.
Leaders allocate the resources needed to achieve desired changes.
Leaders integrate the different changes undertaken into an overall plan.
Leaders project realistic timetables, resources and budgets for a change.

COMMUNICATION AND INVOLVEMENT

Communication

Managers communicate the business reasons for changes.
Managers make a clear case for the need to change.
Managers communicate the big picture of what change is all about.
Managers help people understand what changes are being implemented.
Information is freely available to anyone who needs it.
People understand what is expected of them during the change.
Managers keep people fully informed about changes.

Involvement

Once they understand the general direction of change, people are involved in
    deciding how their particular group or unit will change.
There is give and take about a change before the design is completed.
People are encouraged to say what is on their mind.
Managers are around and available to listen to concerns about change.
Managers seek out and listen to input before going ahead with a decision.
People who express concerns about change are respected.
Doing the right thing is more important than pleasing the boss.

EMPOWERMENT

Enabling Action

Managers provide resources to achieve a change.
Managers delegate responsibility for change appropriately.
Managers include the right people in the change.
Managers stick to their decisions.
Managers make tough decisions in a timely fashion.
Managers act in line with company objectives, not personal agendas.
Managers make decisions based on what people can do, not personal relationships.
Managers support each other and do not undermine top leaders' intentions.
What you know is more important than who you know.

Initiative and Risk Taking

People are not punished for making errors while they learn new ways.
People are willing to take risks for what is important.
Responsibility for outcomes is delegated.
People go beyond their jobs to do what needs to be done.
People are able to make regular decisions about how they do their jobs.
People feel they can make a difference.
People challenge established ways of doing things.
People understand and strive for quality in all work.

LEARNING AND INNOVATION

Willingness to Change

Managers can change course after a change is initiated, if necessary.
Managers are willing to listen to bad news.
Managers are honest with each other.
Managers are willing to change their own ways.
People are willing to change.
Managers are open to feedback about their effectiveness.

Open to Learning

There is an open environment where different ideas can be expressed.
Managers anticipate and plan for future problems and changes.
People receive feedback about their effectiveness at dealing with change.
Managers listen broadly to what is going on in the world.
Managers listen to ideas that are different from their own.
Managers respond quickly to changes in the business environment.
Continual work improvement is a priority.
People have the authority to try out promising new approaches.
People with new ideas get ahead.
People are willing to question traditional ways.
People feel they can learn here.
Innovation is encouraged and rewarded.
People set aside time to improve themselves and do things better.
People periodically review their progress, strengths and weaknesses.
Benchmark the competition; seek data on how the company is doing in relation to other companies.

People Development

Managers coach and develop people.

Managers encourage people to learn and develop their skills.

Managers utilize people's skills and abilities.

People get accurate feedback about their effectiveness.

People get the training they need to implement a change.

Career development is aligned with change.

There are regular opportunities for new learning and skill development.

TEAMWORK

Team Relationships

Teams have the required authority to design and create change.

Teams listen to recommendations from throughout the organization.

Teams provide the necessary resources to implement changes.

Teams give everyone the opportunity to participate in decisions affecting the team.

Teams let individuals know where they stand in terms of their career.

Teams are able to solve problems.

Teams are able to make decisions.

Teams have clear roles.

Teams take responsibility for changes.

Teams have the ability to give and receive information.

Teams share the setting of goals and pathways.

Teams face and work through disagreements fully and openly.

Teams give their people praise and recognition for good work.

Teams show appreciation of each other and avoid sarcasm and put-downs.

Teams are committed to team goals, not their individual agendas.

Teams encourage people to put forth their best efforts.

Teams encourage everyone to say what is on their mind without fear of reprisal.

Team members respect differences among people.

Teams get things done in a timely manner.

When we need to change, people pull together and rise above organizational politics.

There is enough time to get ready for the change.

Teams understand the business reasons for what they do.

Working Across Boundaries

The people who are needed to get a job done are able to work together.
There is cooperation and effective coordination between work groups.
People get things done without interference from other groups.
People deal directly with relevant people in different groups.
People seek out customers and people from related groups and teams.
People can take action to serve customer needs.
People are aware of what customers want.
Other groups can't block us from taking action without good reason.

VALUE PEOPLE

Support and Respect

Managers offer support for people who are facing tough challenges.
Managers avoid blaming individuals for problems.
Managers listen to people's expression of their needs.
Managers understand the impact of changes on their employees.
Managers anticipate and deal supportively with resistance to change.
Managers demonstrate respect for their people.
Managers trust their people to do their best.
Managers avoid using fear and intimidation to motivate people to change.
People know where they stand as change is implemented.
People respect and appreciate each other.
People don't expect others to take advantage of them.
Stress is kept at a manageable level.

Work Spirit

We create an environment where people can do their best work.
Every individual feels their work is important.
People want to work here.
People feel proud of what the organization does.
People feel that the organization accepts what they want to give.
When changes are announced, people expect them to be successful.

ALIGNED POLICIES AND WORK PROCESSES

Work Processes

Red tape does not prevent people from doing what is needed.
Policies and procedures adapt as changes are implemented.
Procedures, policies and structures are flexible when new conditions arise.
Procedures help, not hinder, getting things done.
Policies and expectations for behavior during change are clear.
Layoffs are handled openly and the process for decisions is clear.

Performance Management and Rewards

There are clear and fair negative consequences if you don't participate in a change.
Performance management measures are aligned with change.
There are clear measures of success for the change.
The people who are successful at the change will be rewarded.
Rewards support employee involvement and participation.
Incentives are aligned with change.
Rewards are linked to success at business objectives.
Rewards are aligned with the desired changes.
There are rewards for those who participate in a change.

ACTIVITY 4: Feedback and Action Steps

Analyze Results

Collate and analyze data from different sources. Look for common themes in interviews and focus groups.

You will have rough transcripts (or notes) from each interview and focus group. As much as possible, the transcripts should be arranged within the key factors or themes you select.

The raw data from the survey will be voluminous. The task of the Assessment Team is to boil it down into the most relevant and understandable package. The data can be compared in various ways:

- Individual groups that are part of the organization (defined in any relevant way) can be compared to each other, or to the organization as a whole

- The organization can be compared to a benchmark or comparison organization, or to group norms for high-performing companies

- Group scores may be compared to previous assessments

Prepare the Final Report

Draft a report to the organization utilizing all the data from interviews, focus groups, and surveys.

The strength of the final report is that it combines the hard data from the surveys with the soft data from interviews, focus groups, and open-ended responses from the surveys, that illuminate and add more detail to the areas defined by the survey data.

The data should be arranged according to key points and highlights for each of the key factors. The answers to the open-ended questions from the surveys can be analyzed separately, along with the other soft data from interviews and focus groups.

The creative task of writing an assessment report is to take the data from many sources and summarize it according to key themes.

You should include both general statements of issues and concerns, along with relevant and representative quotes from interviews, focus groups, and open-ended questions.

Draw out key areas for focus and key action steps.

Present Key Findings to the Top Leadership and Change Team

The results are communicated to the top leadership and the Change Team, as well as the organization as a whole. They lead to strategies for overcoming obstacles to change, and a realistic picture of factors that make the organization difficult to change.

The Leadership Team should respond to the assessment first. It is critical that the team planning and implementing change is aware of the internal challenges to change. The data must be presented in detail to this group, and they must plan ways to overcome the key challenges that face the organization in implementing substantive change. This session should be led by an outside facilitator, and should lead to concrete action steps that must be part of the change design.

A similar session should be held with the Change Team as they begin their design process. The data about obstacles should also be included in the various change workshops held throughout the organization.

Responses and discussion by the leadership and Change Teams will lead to the revision and preparation of a summary report with key findings for the whole organization.

Present Summary Results to the Whole Organization

Present summary results at the Individual Change Capability Workshop (page 69) and through other communication forums. They form the basis for an organization-wide discussion of the obstacles to change, and how deeply change must occur in the culture. The results are discussed and assimilated by the key stakeholders involved in the change, and form the foundation for planning how the organization can overcome its internal obstacles to change.

Offer feedback to the organization through discussions of the findings by appropriate groups, starting with the Leadership and Change Teams. Determine a strategy for overcoming organizational obstacles and areas of the culture that need to change. Utilize this picture to inform the visioning and design process.

Data from a specific division, work team, or functional group can be offered in a discussion format, presenting the assessment data referring to that particular group, comparing it to the results from the organization as a whole. This session is important as part of the Employee Involvement Process (page 145) and can be offered later in the change process.

NAVIGATION TOOL:
ASSESSMENT AS A FORUM FOR ACTION

Assessment data is not an end in itself. It is a way to focus the attention of a Change Team or organization on what it must change in order to succeed at the changes it desires. The data concerns issues that must be removed or addressed in order for any change initiative to be successful.

Presenting Feedback Data to Groups

The presentation of data to each part of the organization should be arranged in a discussion format:

- The Assessment Team offers key points in one area only

- The data are presented in graphical format to the group

- Participants can ask questions to make sure they understand

- The presenter becomes a facilitator and asks the participants what they feel are the most important implications of the data. The discussion collects their most important reactions.

- The facilitator asks for key action steps or possible responses for the organization to each area of concern. This is not a decision-making session. The purpose is to get good ideas, not to decide which ones to implement.

- Focus on getting out ideas and prioritizing them, not on making decisions. The facilitator may have to point out that other groups will be meeting, with different ideas, and that no action should be taken until all ideas have been considered.

- Make next steps, or outcomes, of the assessment process clear

- What will happen next in response to the assessment? If nothing happens, people will be demoralized, and their commitment to real change will decline.

GUIDELINES FOR REPORTING ASSESSMENT DATA

■ ***Get feedback out.*** It is important that the Assessment Team see that the data is delivered to the organization. It is especially critical that everyone who has offered information (in an interview, focus group, or survey) get some of the results in return.

There is nothing that so demoralizes or destroys trust and commitment to change as taking information from people and promising them feedback or results, and not getting it to them in a timely manner. This is one of the single most important ways that consultants destroy their own credibility.

■ ***Keep it simple.*** It is an awful experience to drown in data. Keep key points simple and relevant. Include both hard data and examples from interviews, focus groups, and open-ended responses. Report points that are practical and point to areas that can be changed.

While summary reports and briefings should be simple—longer, more detailed reports should be available, especially to the Change Team. The longer reports are important for pinpointing areas to focus attention on in planning the change implementation process.

■ ***Don't argue about methodology.*** One of the commonest ways that organizations deny or avoid the implications of assessment data is by arguing about the methodology.

When you present the data, you should give a summary of how you got the information. Then ask that there not be any further discussion of how the data was gathered. Focus attention on what was found, and whether they find it relevant or not. Not on how you got it.

■ ***Focus on the future, not on blame.*** One of the greatest concerns of leaders, managers, and people is that the assessment data will be used to blame them or their group, or to assess their performance in some way. They feel that if they are found to have difficulties it means they are not performing well. This is a dangerous perception, because it leads people to limit how candid they are, and to offer more bland and rosy information.

Make sure from the beginning that the purpose of discussing the data is to learn and change how the organization is in the future, not on blaming individuals or groups.

The next section, Wave Two: Designing the New Organization, details the key tasks of making the case for change, designing new work processes, the employee involvement process, and aligning systems with new processes.

Wave Two

DESIGNING THE NEW ORGANIZATION

Key Tasks

- *Make the Case for Change*
- *Design New Work Processes and Culture*
- *Employee Involvement Process*
- *Align Systems with New Processes*

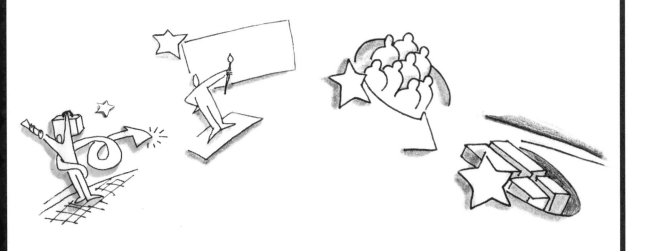

WAVE TWO: INTRODUCTION

After the mobilization phase, the people in the organization should be aligned and ready to change, even if they are also scared, concerned, anxious, and uncertain of where things are leading. The organization has agreed that it needs to undertake a major change in how it does things, and everyone, not just the leaders, has been invited to be a part of the process. New roles—the Change Team, Change Navigator and Change Leader, have been defined and introduced into the organization.

Organizations think of design as creating a plan. A few experts get together and design a perfect way to do things, tell people to change, and then people imperfectly execute the plan. This is the antithesis to how people and organizations really change; this mindset has ruined a majority of change initiatives.

In fact, what works is a design process conducted by a series of feedback loops, where larger groups make input to smaller design teams, who develop increasingly detailed plans. As the plan gets more detailed, more people who will actually change become part of the process. By the time the plan is ready for full implementation, no person should be in the dark about what is to be expected, and no person should not have had some opportunity to participate in the process.

The processes in Wave Two are even more interlocking and simultaneous than those of Wave One. While change begins with a mandate and communication from the top, the Change Team is involved in a collaborative design process that includes a Council of Employees, several subteams who are working on parts of the process, and a human resources design team that is looking at the support structures for employee performance. The leadership and Change Team are less the experts who design the new paths, but the coordinators of many simultaneous design and information processes.

The first step, Make the Case for Change, is detailed in Task 1.

TASK 1: MAKE THE CASE FOR CHANGE

Key Activities

■ *Communicate the Need to Change*

■ *Leverage Commitment from the Top*

■ *Ensure Middle Management Support for the Change*

■ *Oversee the Change Designs*

SETTING THE COURSE

When the design process is initiated, the leader's involvement has barely begun. Just saying "Go ahead," won't lead to change—the vested interests of the status quo, and the fears of moving into the unknown, can slow the organization to a halt. As the organization begins to redesign itself, the leader must exert constant pressure—encouraging, rewarding, setting boundaries, and keeping the core message in front of people.

After a change is announced, people wait to read the "tea leaves" to see if it is real. The leader must make this clear, and steer everyone in the organization into the role they must take. In addition to showing up, everywhere, the leadership must make the case for change dramatically and continuously, coach people toward commitment and set the overall values that will determine the change. The overall objective of this wave is to achieve total organizational commitment to the change, with everyone sharing in the excitement and the accountability for the results.

Core Activities

Outcomes

- Convey the Leadership Team's drive and intense commitment to change throughout the organization in a way that builds employees' and mangers' desire to create the needed results, and sustains action through full implementation cycle.

- Increase the whole organization's undersanding of the complexity of change, and the need for active engagement by everyone

- Develop employee (and other stakeholder) understanding and commitment to a change through a vigorous, active, and visible communication strategy, including the use of large group communication sessions

- Executives are perceived as intensely involved with the change initiative and seen as "one of us," rather than "one of them"

- A persuasive story about "why we have to change" that can be readily communicated to the organization

- A plan for well-designed, high impact communication processes to create top-down and bottom-up information flows

- All employees know the reason for the change, their role in the change, and what it will mean for them

- Executives know how well the change initiatives are progressing, and have ways to track momentum

Continuity and Variation

People need to know what they can hold on to, what won't change, in order to be comfortable making radical change. There needs to be clarity about what is changing and what will stay the same. This allows people a sense of psychological security. Without it, few will take risks. In most current change, what remains has to do with deep company values and a vision for the future, rather than with the continuation of past work processes or relationships. It takes considerable work to generate excitement about things that are more abstract when people are losing things that are concrete and immediate.

Create Opportunities for Action

As processes, roles and structures are expected to change, people feel powerless. While some will "grab the authority in the air," most will simply wait. This produces an unhealthy, passive work atmosphere. People need to learn what decisions they can make, and what they can do to be part of change. Clichés won't do—people need concrete specifics.

Confusion about Scope and Boundaries

Change breaks down boundaries, realigns work groups and business units, and creates lots of disconnections in the organization. People, however, need to know clearly where their work begins and ends, and how to work with other groups. The leaders have to keep making the boundary shifts clear, so people won't become confused, demoralized or angry. Unclear boundaries cause conflict, anxiety and confusion. People need boundaries if they are to experiment with new ways of working. When departmental boundaries and role definitions change radically, people feel insecure.

Model Credibility

Leaders have to get clear as to what they can and cannot promise in attempting to maintain some stability during the change process. Some tend to over-promise: "This is the final layoff." Others under-commit and share little or no information. The key to keeping people committed to change is leadership credibility, which can only be maintained by telling the truth. People know the truth anyway, but when a leader tells it first or directly, everyone is relieved.

People will not really be convinced that the change will happen if they don't see any high-level support for it. People in organizations are unusually sensitive to the examples of the behavior of the leaders, not what they say. If they say, for example, that they want to hear from the people involved, and then schedule a short meeting to share only the sketchiest details of the plans, people will conclude that their input isn't wanted.

GUIDING PRINCIPLES

■ *Focus on the big picture.* Even if people agree on the need to change, they often hear different messages about what this means. The process of making the case for change involves leaders setting up a deep and full picture of what is being proposed, why, and how it will happen. Instead of just telling people what will happen, leaders often have to lead people through the learning process to discover how change must happen, and where it will lead. One critical element of top leadership is their ability to tell a good story about the change, the other is to utilize stategic illustration to create a "roadmap" of the change process. The leader links the current crises and the vision of change to help the organization develop the capacity to overcome them.

■ *Keep everyone on purpose.* The leader has to keep people focused on the objectives, even as immediate pressures intervene. Too often people get so involved in a change, they stop seeing that the change may not answer the purpose for which it is intended, and they do not feel that the organization is open to hearing about this. This "Emperor's New Clothes" phenomenon means that the organization is on a path that is contrary to many people's views.

Leaders need to ensure that those implementing change remain in touch with the true purpose of the change, and do not lose it through being too involved in the details or because they think it is "done" before it is truly complete. As the change unfolds, it is up to the leaders to stay in touch, and periodically check whether what is being implemented is what was intended. Sometimes many people have doubts or concerns, but until the leadership opens up the topic, or ask what people feel, they remain silent. Sometimes the rush to implement covers up real issues or factors that have been lost sight of.

■ *Teach, don't preach.* Leaders often see change leadership as telling people what to do; they suffer from the delusion that commanding change will create success. This often means that people get the message to do but not to think. The leader must make a case that makes it clear why the organization has to change, the general direction change will take, what is expected from people, and the desired outcomes. The leader should not prescribe how or what people should do, but should allow many different groups, starting with the Change Team, to work together to discover the best ways. The leader needs to give up the idea that he knows more and better than everyone—due to urgency to get people moving.

■ ***Use all available media for communication—not just print.*** The process of communication must be continual, ongoing and personal. People often do not get the message the first time, or need to hear about change in different ways. They hear the words, but they might not connect change with their own behavior.

Personal contact is particularly valuable. Large interactive meetings can model doing business in new ways and streamline process. Preparing for these small group discussions (brown bag lunches, breakfasts, coffees) can get executives into direct contact with different layers of the organization in an informal setting.

Leaders need to appreciate both aspects of communication:

Content: the data, the facts

Compassion: the human side, connecting personally, letting people know you "feel" too

Many managers focus excessively on the contents, and view communication as the process of sharing facts or information. In situations where change is difficult for many people, the human side is often more important than "the facts." People need support for their feelings in order to stay committed to the process.

Communication is not only about the message itself. Your people are looking for cues to what you really feel, want and will do. If you do not back up your communication with real actions—supporting people to change, rewarding those who are involved in the effort, listen to what people say, and spending time on change yourself, then people will discount your message. They are looking for congruence.

Strategic illustration can be a potent vehicle for creating a "roadmap" that can be used over the long run to communicate milestones and changes in direction. Creating a picture of the process can provide a way to get people to understand and support the change.

KEY ACTIVITIES FOR TASK 1

ACTIVITY 1: Communicate the Need to Change

Leaders should continually help all parts of the organization understand why they need to change, and how they can change. The leaders should be alert to pointing out current difficulties or dissatisfaction with underlying change. The negative consequences of continuing business as usual should be dramatized.

The need for change and the nature of the response must be communicated in a series of interactive sessions, with a small enough group, usually team by team, to allow for discussion. If it is an important change, a top leader should come to talk in person—presence communicates seriousness.

While taking care not to blame individuals for the current state (after all, they were the leaders), they should make it clear that there is no choice not to change. The only way to vote against change, unless there is an explicit role for loyal opposition to it, is to leave.

The leaders can keep information coming into the organization. In addition to information about the need to change, the leaders can gather information about other successful experiments in change, outside heroes who have been part of successful change. Even better, leaders can bring key leaders with them to visit other companies. As a leader, you should make it your business to seek out other examples and models of change. As a leader, you have your own blind spots, and seeing other examples and talking to other leaders will help you see beyond them.

Put in place and participate in processes for upward communication from all levels across the organization. Visibly listen and respond to the input. Ensure that a wide range of media are used.

Keep the whole organization involved. Executives should participate in the Individual Change Capacity Workshop (Task 3) to demonstrate their personal involvement and commitment to the change initiative, so that people feel that their leaders truly "walk the talk." Leaders must be sure that they show up at these events to dialogue, to listen to concerns and become aware of considerations that must be taken into account, not to sell their ideas or solve employee problems. Listen and ask questions.

Make sure that you agree to get back in touch with people with responses to their concerns. Keep your promises promptly. Your response is important to them; not getting back can do more to demoralize not just the person involved, but everyone that person comes into contact with.

NAVIGATION TOOL:
TELL THE STORY OF THE CHANGE

While the general fact of change has already been shared, and people know that it will happen, one of the most important activities of the top leadership is to help the organization understand the "story" of the change.

The Change Leader must not only give the facts, but must offer them in a dramatic, clearly understandable story that people can understand, care about and share with others.

Like any good story, the change story should tell people:

- Why this is happening

- Who are the key players in the upcoming changes

- The impact on us, and how it will be handled

- The core values, what will remain unchanged, despite the pressures

- A vision of the future, what we can become that is exciting

- The problems we will face, and how everyone will be involved

- The task ahead, and what is expected of everyone

The leader should carefully craft the Change Story offering the following information, clearly, fully, and repeatedly to various parts of the organization, with an opportunity for exchange and discussion. If all the answers are not clear yet, the leadership should at least offer guidelines to how the process will go, or how the decision will be made, and when.

The story has several elements, including:

- What is changing around us?

- What are the implications of these changes for us?

- What generally have we decided to change, and why?

- What concrete outcomes and goals do we hold, and how will we evaluate success?

- Who will implement and be affected by the change?

- What are the implications of the change for job security, employment and the need for employee skills?

- How will everyone participate in the change?

- What will not change (such as values and current programs)?

- How will people be kept informed?

- What will we keep in place?

ACTIVITY 2: Leverage Commitment from the Top

Build commitment through connecting to critical stakeholders—those people who can make or break the process:

- Identify the critical stakeholders

- Communicate personally with them

Arrange personal time with key stakeholders, and do more than just ask them to be committed. Solicit their concerns; ask them about reservations. See what they need to make the change successful. Decide what will be done with people who you suspect are not being fully candid, or who are openly not on board.

Expect that there will be "loyal opposition" with regard to the particular kind of change. If people can't disagree openly, they will do it in secret, and you will not hear about their concerns, and the organization simply won't change. (If not, this must be communicated, along with a time frame and the consequences of not being on board.) There may need to be a period of time during which everything can be challenged and all assumptions fully debated after which people are either on board or out.

Interact among the Leadership Team to check on the progress of the communication process with all critical stakeholders: establish a group picture of the broader commitment to change. Where there are issues or problems, address them quickly.

Only the top leadership can minimize turf battles and politics around change. The politics may not be open. People may let the design phase happen, assuming that the steam will go out of the effort before it begins. That is why opposition sometimes doesn't surface until implementation.

ACTIVITY 3: Ensure Middle Management Support for the Change

Combine individual communication with the "critical few" with large-group interactive sessions. This process will be described in Task 3, the Employee Involvement Process. Management needs the information and motivation to articulately promote the change.

Develop meaningful roles for middle management to participate in leading change.

Periodically check on the mindset and actions through skip level communication sessions with individuals and groups outside of your regular reporting structure.

ACTIVITY 4: Oversee the Change Designs

Leaders must walk a line between micromanagement and detachment. They must set clear expectations, goals and parameters for the desired changes, if possible with the involvement of the Change Team. Then they have to back off and let the team work.

However, they will want to exercise oversight and be briefed frequently. They should have regular interaction with the Design Team and with the key elements of the organization that will be changing, to know what is happening, and to ask what they can do to help.

Their task is to provide integration, and to keep people focused on the big picture, while they increasingly move into more detailed levels. The leaders should ask tough questions, but not seek to get involved, or even critique, every specific of the plan. If the Change Team gets into the practice of having to check every detail with the top team, you will have created another dysfunctional process that will reverberate throughout the organization, negating your verbal efforts to empower people. Your concern is to keep people focused on outcomes and deliverables, to trust them to discover how to get to them, and how to mobilize the whole organization into new directions.

Top leaders also have to be alert and ready to get involved in cases of conflict between groups. You have to make sure that conflicts are not avoided, as they often point to difficult issues. You also have to step in if an individual is obstructing or blocking efforts. The Change Team or Change Leader often doesn't have the authority to stop this.

The next step is to design new work processes and cultures as shown in Task 2.

TASK 2: DESIGN NEW WORK PROCESSES AND CULTURE

Key Activities:

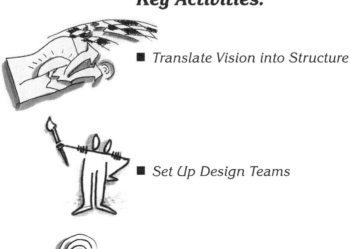

- *Translate Vision into Structure*

- *Set Up Design Teams*

- *Integrate Designs into Overall Plan*

SETTING THE COURSE

The task of designing the new organization, and a plan for implementing it is huge and complex. While this guide cannot do justice to the whole process of organizational redesign, we will give you an overview. To illuminate this element of the change process, we will offer two perspectives on organizational design: the general elements of the new organization structures that are emerging, and how the Change Team can do their work with enough connection and involvement of the rest of the organization to lead to a successful outcome.

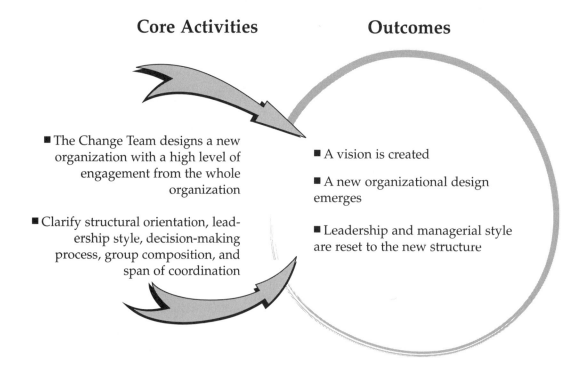

Core Activities

- The Change Team designs a new organization with a high level of engagement from the whole organization

- Clarify structural orientation, leadership style, decision-making process, group composition, and span of coordination

Outcomes

- A vision is created

- A new organizational design emerges

- Leadership and managerial style are reset to the new structure

CHALLENGES

Understand the Many Levels of Change

In every industry, organizations are changing to new structures that are capable of fast change. Several types of change are leading to the need to shift organization. Each of these adds to the need to change, and to the capacity of organizations to operate differently:

- **Global Competition**
    - Speed of changes in the marketplace
    - Need to cut costs
    - Customer pressure, specialized niche markets
    - Shift to global markets, heightened competition

- **New Information Systems**
    - Availability of systems to give everyone access to information at once
    - New technology that places greater demands on people to respond
    - Tendency for dispersed, virtual organizations

- **Desire for Meaning at Work**
    - Employees want more autonomy, more discretion, more task variety, and more coherence in their work
    - Employees want meaningful work and to make decisions
    - Employees desire to learn, grow, and develop capabilities

These changes demand changes in the structure and design of every type of organization. These changes lead to organizational designs with processes and structures where people do whole tasks, have authority to respond directly to customers, work across boundaries on multiple tasks and responsibilities, and have responsibility for bigger jobs rather than a part of a part of a job.

The critique of functional organizations has been that they depersonalize and limit people's ability to innovate and respond to external changes and customer demands, leading people to lose their motivation over time. So some designs that seem rational may backfire in practice, because they do not provide structures people want to work in. As the nature of tasks is more discretionary, and demands more skills and abilities in people, some of the more traditional structures are becoming less effective.

Clarify the Vision and Pathways to Change

With so much change, it is far from obvious what needs to be changed, how and what people should be doing. The pace, scope and urgency of change leads people to begin to develop ad hoc structures to respond to individual crises, and makes it difficult to find the time and energy to step back and create an organization that works. People spend more and more time inventing ways to get the job done.

The direction of major changes in organizations is to build adaptive and flexible organizations that allow individuals to respond to needs quickly, but also provide support for sharing information, getting large projects done, and aligning vast numbers of people, often in many places, to understand what is important.

The method of developing this alignment is to create broad agreement on what people are trying to do and why. People in every part of the organization have a shared understanding of what their purpose is, and why they are doing it. They can then understand how their own group and individual work fits in with the overall goals.

Also, the organization is not static, but forms a moving target continually changing and evolving. But it can't do everything; and it needs to focus its efforts. The creation of an organizational vision is one way to begin the process of change. Until there is a shared commitment to a particular destination, that is clear to all, the organization cannot design new ways to get there. The process of organizational change cannot proceed without a vision.

There are many levels of vision. There is a large overall purpose, strategic intent and direction that is set by the top leaders of the organization. This is the overall vision and mission. But this is understandably somewhat vague and intangible. The Change Team must create a vision of the outcome of the change, fitting into the broad organizational vision, and then begin a process to rethink the organization to move toward this vision.

The vision of change is the destination. It needs to fit the overall purpose, and provide inspiration and focus to the activity of many people. It is not designed entirely by the Change Team, but rather is put together out of many activities involving many people. The creation of the change vision, and the new organizational design, comes from Task 3, the Employee Involvement Process.

From the Pyramid to the Circle

We are in the midst of an evolution in organizational structure, which broadly can be defined as a shift from the traditional, hierarchical, functionally designed organization structure, toward a model that is flatter, based on small, more loosely coupled units, that are more immediately responsive to the customer and the external environment.

The major recent issue in organizational design has been the discovery that the highly functional, activity-based structures, now called "silos," have many drawbacks where the issues are speed of change, closeness to the customer, and quality. The issue is how to link the different functional groups, and the experimentation with different forms of looser, more flexible types of linkage. The use of cross-functional councils, task forces and other representative groups as a design alternative should be presented. Then the issue is not, for example, to shift from a functional- to a horizontal-based structure, but how to link groups so that there is more informal contact at more levels of the organization. The desire is not to form groups where the integration is accomplished by a group at the next higher level, as it is in the functional organization, but to do it informally, quickly, and at the lowest appropriate level.

The reasons for this shift has to do with the tremendous rate of change in the environment today. The functional model was not designed to be able to change, and was not flexible or responsive to change. The newer models are more able to change. Today's efforts at team-based organizations, toward total quality, reengineering, and even of drastic cost cutting and eliminating of layers and middle management personnel, can all be seen as aspects of this greater shift.

Most broadly, the evolution is from the functional, hierarchical to a more process-oriented, horizontal, customer-focused model.

The two models can be contrasted in the table on page 136.

Functional Organization Characteristics	Networked Organization Characteristics

Specialization
    Tight boundaries
    Experts grouped together
    Specialized careers
	Intimacy with Stakeholders/Customers
	    Customer-oriented
	    Problem-solving focus
	    Cross-functional teams

Formal Relationships
    Clear chain of command
    Defined roles
    Rules, regulations, policies, procedures
    Reporting relationships
	Flexibility
	    Changing job definitions
	    Shifting team composition
	    Aligned by values and vision
	    Leadership according to task

Centralization
    Control from the top
    Profit and loss for whole enterprise
    Top managers have decision authority
	Small Clusters
	    Shared control
	    Each business has customer and P&L responsibility
	    Unit makes decisions within parameters

One Right Way
    Keep repeating model
    Tradition
    Do it our way only
	Fluid , Adaptive, Learning
	    Keep experimenting
	    Decision by data
	    See what works

Organizational Structure Evolution: From Pyramid To Circle

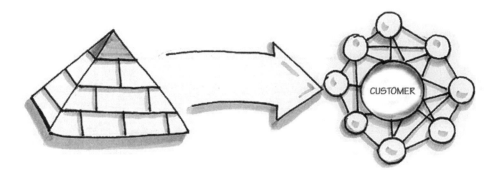

The different design alternatives can be arrayed on a continuum, with qualities shifting as in the chart below:

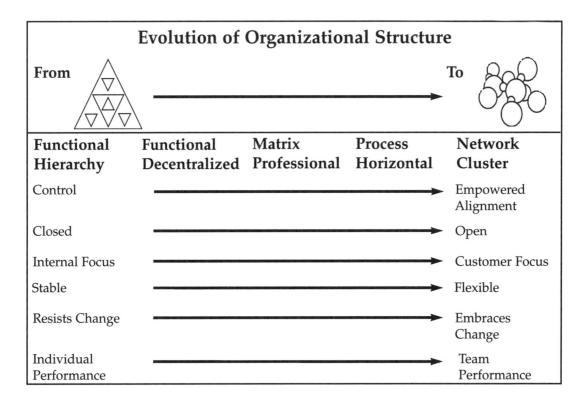

From				To
Functional Hierarchy	**Functional Decentralized**	**Matrix Professional**	**Process Horizontal**	**Network Cluster**
Control				Empowered Alignment
Closed				Open
Internal Focus				Customer Focus
Stable				Flexible
Resists Change				Embraces Change
Individual Performance				Team Performance

New Design Criteria: Processes that Add Customer Value

The redesign of the organization moves from the functional organization that is stable and organized around control from the top. The newer organization models are horizontal, with shifting, cross-functional, cross-boundary teams enacting processes that relate to providing value to customers. This process design has been the subject of hundreds of new management books in the past decade, and we will not go into the basics of this here.

The design process asks the Change Team to question major parts of the way the organization works and runs, in favor of providing greater value, more quickly and flexibly, to various customers. Everything about the organization can be broken up and put together in a new way to follow this imperative.

Several challenges follow from this insight. First, unlike the traditional pyramid, where a small group designed and controlled processes for the whole, the new organization is one where many people contribute. The new design may set some new pathways for the organization, but it will not be the end point of a new pyramid. The design must include elements that allow people to reconsider and change elements of the design. But it cannot be questioned by everyone all the time; it would be another ad hoc attempt to give customers what they wanted, without increasing the organization's ability to satisfy the next customer.

The Employee Involvement Process (page 145) goes hand in hand with the redesign, because it is the pathway to engage everyone, including customers, in an inquiry into how the organization can achieve its vision. The Change Team must consider itself the steward for change in the whole organization, not as an arm of the leadership who has delegated them responsibility for deciding the nature of change.

Teams and Work Groups Themselves Need to Rethink the Purposes of Their Structures and Processes

The key activities define the internal design of the structure of a work unit. The individual team members, who are closest to their work, need to rethink the key elements that make up the structure of their work group or team, and the implications and rationale for making different choices in each area. If they do it, under the guidance of the Change Team and Change Navigator, they will own it. The Change Team coaches them, offers resources, gives general directions, but does not specify everything about the design.

Generally, a work group or team, will be making design decisions that reflect the new focus of their organization. However, different work groups have different concerns, environmental situations, and overall organizational styles, which will also influence the decisions around structure.

A word about the use of the term "work group" or "work team." Generally, the distinction between the terms has to do with the degree that the people in a group do different work individually (work group), and all report to one supervisor, or work together on a task (work team). To the extent that they work together, or have different capabilities but are working toward a shared goal, they are a team. On the continuum from work group to team, there are a range of types of groups. These differences will be explored later in this activity.

In this phase, the Change Team shifts their focus from the strategic level to the design of the internal structure of the business unit and each work group.

Key choices focus on establishing where on the continuum between functional and networked organizations. What leads this choice is clarity about the functions that the organization has to accomplish. There is no one perfect model. It is common to have a hybrid organization of functional, divisional, and project-based clusters. The function that the organization needs to accomplish influences its form.

The Change Navigator Will be Called on Increasingly to Help an Organization Shift its Structure and Design Model

The Change Navigator will need to push for a strong clarification of the function of the organization. Because organizational design is in the midst of a rennaisance, many people have had limited experience with anything other than the functional, hierarchial model. They cannot believe that people can be accountable without supervisors. The Change Navigator will need to serve as a credible resource for examples of other organizational forms. It is often helpful to visit organizations which are using new models to gather first-hand experience.

The Navigator is also experienced in leading large groups, and in helping to coordinate large-scale changes that involve a smaller team—the Change Team and the leadership team, working with the other parts of the organization. The Change Navigator is the guide who puts together the various elements of the process, making sure they are done in a relevant sequence, aligned with the desired outcome.

KEY ACTIVITIES FOR TASK 2

ACTIVITY 1: Translate Vision into Structure

In this activity, the Change Team must work intensively with the data it has obtained, to move from the broad general vision, to set a specific critical path for the organization. The design process involves setting some key paths and milestones for the change process.

First, the Change Team must set the overall level of change. Once more, it checks to see that the change desired fits the external changes, and the level of change the organization needs. It integrates all the data, and puts it together into a Roadmap, that puts the change into a whole context. The Roadmap is a detailed, strategic illustration that shows all elements of the desired change. The map shows the whole picture, and then the team must set specifics and desired outcomes. Everyone thinks they are changing all the time; the organization needs some specific outcomes to determine the success of change. Just financial measures, such as lower costs, are not enough. Many change efforts simply cut costs without growing capability or changing the way people work.

The team must make several types of design and structure choices.

How Will the Work Group or Unit Interface with the Customer and the Other Groups External to It?

The choices are to structure the unit to focus on a particular Activity (function), or a particular Product (output) or Customer. The choice of interface is also about whether the unit is a part of a group of units each doing a different function—e.g., marketing, research and development, manufacturing, sales, customer service—or whether the unit is part of a group with a responsibility to satisfy a customer group or take responsibility for a single product.

These choices are usually made on an enterprise level. The Change Team or design consultants may, however, point out to top management an incongruence between the chosen structure and the needs of the enterprise for the demands of the environment. But they must look to the top management group for validation of their choice.

How will a Support Group Relate to its Internal Customer?

Only line groups really have the option to organize by activity, product or customer. Service or support groups do not, except in a much broader sense. Support groups are those activities that support the work of line groups, such as human resources, legal, information systems, customer service, and procurement. There is a structural choice for such groups, and that is whether the participants of these specialized functions are dedicated to a line group, or part of a centralized functional group that offers services to the line. Today, there is much movement to make support staff people part of process teams, and less connected to their service center. Thus, human resources, marketing, legal and information services people are becoming part of work groups, not resources that come from a central office.

The Change Team must also set up the Design Process, that links to top leadership, including the Change Leader, must be developed, as well as a series of links to the rest of the organization, that will be described more fully in Task 3. There are different levels of employee involvement. Setting up the Employee Involvement Council, and various communication methods and pathways will keep everybody informed.

ACTIVITY 2: Set Up Design Teams

The Change Team cannot do the design alone. Every major design effort involves the creation of various Design Teams, which focus on different parts of the change. Each of these teams will have a set scope of change, and will probably have a Change Team member leading that team. The teams work independently, but the Change Team will need to have regular, usually weekly, meetings to report on what each team is doing, and integrate their efforts.

There are many detailed ways to go about the overall redesign process. Our concern in this guide is to map the processes of employee involvement, not to offer a guide on how to conduct reengineering or redesign.

ACTIVITY 3: Integrate Designs into Overall Plan

The end phase of this task is to get the different Design Teams together, to present their designs, and to integrate them into a whole. Usually this process is done with the Change Leader and other members of the leadership team overseeing. The presentations are a time of discussion and careful exploration of the links, implications and outcomes of each plan.

The designs are then shared with the rest of the organization, often using a large-group meeting process, where many or even all the people who are affected by a change come together for an intensive workshop to explore the changes and the Employee Involvement Process (page 145).

Now plans must be designed for the implementation process. As in the design process, the design of the implementation path should be by the team or unit that will be responsible for it, under the guidance of the Change Team.

TASK 3: EMPLOYEE INVOLVEMENT PROCESS

Key Activities

■ *Identify Stakeholder Groups*

■ *Develop Employee Involvement Process*

SETTING THE COURSE

This task focuses on creating a strong, vital process of dialogue between all the employees who are involved in creating a sustainable change, and is conducted to interlock with the other levels of Wave Two.

The objective here is designed to make sure that everyone in the organization is involved and engaged in planning change, not just a small elite group. The effectiveness of these activities represents an up-front investment that will speed up the path to implementation, and ensure the eventual success of change efforts.

The Change Team implements a process to communicate to stakeholder groups the purpose, goals, approach and steps of the change initiative, and an involvement process to promote exchange about a change and build commitment to it.

The activities for this set of objectives continually and repeatedly are designed to seek out and engage every person, inside the organization and outside, who is affected by the change, refining and assessing the concerns about change of employees and external stakeholders.

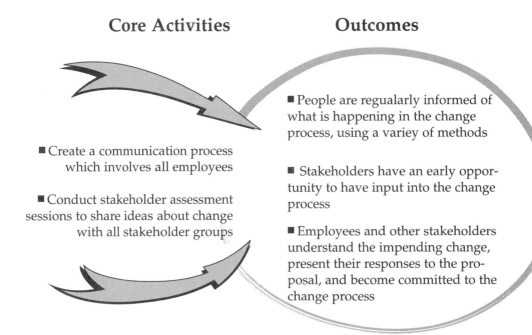

Core Activities

- Create a communication process which involves all employees

- Conduct stakeholder assessment sessions to share ideas about change with all stakeholder groups

Outcomes

- People are regualarly informed of what is happening in the change process, using a variey of methods

- Stakeholders have an early opportunity to have input into the change process

- Employees and other stakeholders understand the impending change, present their responses to the proposal, and become committed to the change process

CHALLENGES

Change Affects Everyone Differently

Different stakeholders—employees who are affected by or involved in the change—have different needs, agendas and understanding of what will happen in the change process. They often work at cross-purposes or undermine each other. Misunderstandings need to be cleared up as soon as possible.

Many people in an organization are affected by a change initiative. Change can be significantly slowed, or undermined, if members of various affected groups lack understanding or commitment to the change.

The Change Team needs to design ongoing processes to keep various groups in the loop and to mediate issues as they arise. They need to monitor this continually, not as a one-time event.

Change affects every corner of the organization, aspects of which may remain undetected until problems arise later on. The Change Team or the leadership is not able to anticipate every effect or wrinkle of a proposed change. Listening to the feedback of the people who have to carry out the work is important before the change is solidified. The issues that are raised are too often dismissed as examples of resistance, rather than issues to be worked on in the change. Impatience once again leads to unexpected outcomes that undermine the desired results.

Surfacing Hidden Information

People involved in a change often have important information about the change they do not share until they are brought into the process. The members of the Change Team often are not aware of certain aspects of the work processes they are changing, and they therefore embark on their design with incomplete information. The people who do the work also know many ways to make impactful changes ("quick hits") and what changes can have real impact. This input is sometimes of higher quality than carefully done studies by the Change Team or a consultant.

Need for Continual Communication

The process of defining, contacting, and involving stakeholders should begin at the very outset of the change process. Stakeholders should be involved in planning all communication and dialogue about change. It should have many loops and be fully mutual, with many opportunities for exchange and give-and-take.

The more time that elapses before a stakeholder group is involved, the greater the chance of destructive rumors, lowered morale, anger and misperception about the change.

The involvement process is an ongoing process. Stakeholder groups should be contacted and involved regularly in the process.

In a large change initiative, it is best to create an Employee Involvement Council representing the different groups affected by the change, that is coordinated with the Change Team and the Leadership Team.

Short-Circuit Energy Drains

If proposed changes are not communicated directly, rumors, misunderstandings, fears and misinformation will undermine performance, and tie up much needed energy. In a vacuum, people fill up the absence of information with their worst fears. The desire to wait to tell people about a change is really a defense by the consultants to avoid hearing bad news, and should be indulged with caution. The Change Team should encourage the organization to put out too much, not too little information, and let people pick what they want. Even drafts and work in progress should be shared.

Balance Speed with Involvement

The Change Team needs to balance the need to include people with the need for speed. While time is of the essence, and you cannot get everybody involved in everything, there is nonetheless a tendency to move too quickly, and not stop and take time to see if the employees are on board. Deadline and schedule pressure causes consultants to forget to check in, and leads to plans without understanding or commitment.

Impatience and the desire to get on with it lead the Change Team or the Change Navigator to neglect to cover all bases, leading to trouble later on. Impatience and deadline pressure may speed up a process today, but it leads to rework and longer time to implement later. The more time is spent in building commitment and understanding up-front, the less time it takes to get people on board to change.

GUIDING PRINCIPLES

■ ***Build a critical mass of people by including people early in the process.***
You need to focus on getting a critical mass of people on board, rather than focusing too much time on the detractors.

■ **Communication builds commitment.** Before stakeholders can commit to change they must be fully informed about the change. Communication is an essential ingredient to promote employee involvement and, therefore, enhances the potential success of the change initiative.

The employee involvement process is designed to involve, through direct communication and exchange, the people who will be affected by the change, helping them become enrolled in the effort, understand its aims and intent, and become involved in making the change work.

■ ***High employee involvement represents an up-front commitment that has a later payoff.*** The more thoroughly this is done early in the process, the fewer difficulties and, therefore, the less time the change will take to implement.

While an extensive communication and employee involvement process takes time, and may slow or even cause rethinking of some elements of a proposed change, in the end, it makes the process of implementation and achieving real results quicker and more certain.

■ ***Commitment emerges out of dialogue, not out of one-way communication.***
The process of moving commitment to change through the organization must be rooted in meaningful and self-critical exchange between the different stakeholder groups, and the Leadership and Change Teams. Information when not accompanied by exchange and direct communication will not have much effect. It will either inspire a backlash, misunderstandings, or have the effect of alienating people from the change process, rather than enrolling them.

■ *Inclusion of all employees does not mean you need to achieve consensus.* While inclusion and listening are critical to building commitment to change, the process of exchange and communication is not to be confused with consensus. At times change needs to be done without getting everybody fully committed, although it is helpful to invite everybody once or twice to get on board.

■ *Change Teams must be open and permeable and include as many people as possible.* Find creative ways to include many people. Use sub-teams, task forces, town hall meetings, brief surveys, video-conferencing, and e-mail. Be creative! Provide multiple opportunities for input, while ensuring the input does not slow the whole change. Bringing in new players helps drive the change to completion. New members on a team will be a useful exercise. Their resistance, excitement and concerns will mirror those of the organization. Use it to learn.

KEY ACTIVITIES OF TASK 3

ACTIVITY 1: Identify Stakeholder Groups

Identify and begin to access the level of impact and commitment to the change process of each group that will potentially be affected by it (stakeholders), and their specific concerns. The Stakeholder Map will be used by the Change Team to create an enrollment and involvement strategy for each group, and create various sub-teams to aid the design effort.

Identify and list all of the key internal functional groups and task teams that will be affected by the change. This should be done in draft form in the initial phases of the engagement:

- As a prelude to the development of the design that identifies resources required for the change

- To help identify members of the Employee Involvement Council who will plan and coordinate the implementation of the involvement effort

For the purposes of this task, a stakeholder group is defined as an employee work group or team that shares a set of functional responsibilities and a perspective on change. They usually work together, or nearby, and have regular contact with each other. In most cases, a stakeholder group should not contain more than 30 people, and more than two levels of the organization.

Identify stakeholder groups both within and external to the organization. This is more than a list of functional groups that are affected; it includes those who are indirectly or peripherally involved in the change process.

- Change support groups (finance, human resources)
- Middle managers
- Unions
- Customers
- Suppliers
- Owners and stockholders

Stakeholders are made up of internal voices as well as external voices—such as customers, community members, families, suppliers, and strategic alliances—who are affected by or who affect the change.

Establish who they are and begin to consider what the change will mean to them. While you begin by trying to imagine the effect of the change on them, you must be sure that all of your hunches are verified directly through your interaction with each stakeholder group in face-to-face meetings. Or, to jump start this process, you can invite representatives of each of these groups to a large group session of 100+ people. Seat participants at round tables in a mixture of all representatives. At table groups have them discuss their thoughts, feelings, attitudes, expectations and information they have about the proposed change. The goal is not to give them information—which they should be told will follow—but to listen to their perspective and concerns. This process can also be done in face-to-face interviews, using the Stakeholder Map on the next page.

Assess the level of ownership of each group:

What percentage of the group is:

- Advocates of change
- Fence-sitters, not sure
- Opposed to the change
- Misinformed or unclear about what will happen

Assess how each group is experiencing the change:

- Are they in denial, resistance, exploring implications, or committed to it?

Explore how they want to be involved and what they can offer or need from the change.

Note: Do not try to get the most negative people on board at first. People change over time, and even if they begin negatively, they may accept the change over time. Recognize that people get upset about change, and feel threatened about it at first, and that is a natural reaction. Let the process of stakeholder enrollment evolve over time.

NAVIGATION TOOL:
STAKEHOLDER MAP

Fill in the map with your initial thoughts, which then can be developed as group input is gathered.

Stakeholder Map Planning Tool				
Stakeholder Group	Amount of Impact (High, Med., Low)	Key Concerns	Importance to the Change (High, Med., Low)	Commitment to Level (High, Med., Low)

The map should include thoughts about how the groups might be affected by the change, their attitude and perspective, their concerns, possible obstacles they may pose to the change process, and the key people who represent that group.

To discover what the stakeholders know, what they want to know, and how they understand what the change means to them, assess each stakeholder group according to the following matrix:

Stakeholder Strategy Matrix

		Commitment Level		
		High	**Medium**	**Low**
Amount of Impact	**High**	Address concerns directly	Involve	Enlist their help
	Medium	Involve	Involve	Inform
	Low	Keep Informed	Keep Informed	Infrom as Needed

Fill in the name of each stakeholder group where it belongs in the matrix.

Focus your attention especially on low-commitment, high-impact groups. These are the stakeholders that are most important to success.

You need to design activities to get them involved in the change. Design ways to get those with low commitment, or those who are against the change, or have the most to lose by it, involved in the process.

The low-commitment, low-impact group needs to be kept abreast of change, but is not seeking further involvement in change planning.

The high-commitment, high-impact group are your firm allies, and you should enlist their help in the change process, perhaps to help the low-commitment groups get on board. The high-commitment, low-impact group should be called upon as needed.

ACTIVITY 2: Develop Employee Involvement Process

Create an Employee Involvement Council, a cross-sectional, cross-level group representing all of the stakeholders of the change process, that creates a two-way communication conduit for the Change Team. This team conducts a systematic exchange with various elements of the organization about the nature of the change and the impacts and effects of the change on each group. The purpose of this process is to build connection to the change process, and commitment to it by each affected group.

The council meets regularly to:

- Identify and raise issues concerning the change to the Change Team

- Disseminate information about the change through the organization

- Guide the process of dialogue about the change within the organization

- Help stakeholders elect or appoint additional members to the council. Assure that all recruited members have a clear sense of the mission, and have time and energy to fulfill their commitment.

- Help the team come together using team building, and facilitate a process of defining their task with the Change Team

Call the stakeholder group leaders at least monthly to solicit questions, new concerns, and ask how they are doing. Conduct follow-up meetings before implementation, and repeat major elements of the design, with new information about the implementation process. Facilitate problem-solving and connection processes between stakeholders and the Change Team as an ongoing communication clarifier.

Coach and work with individual stakeholders and groups who have special problems or difficulties, or need further support and resources in order to become involved in the change.

Implement and cascade communication and exchange about the change through the organization, getting input from all stakeholders.

Design a communication strategy using various communications media, including meetings, forums, newsletters, memos, informal discussion, videos and hotlines, to build ongoing communication about change through the organization, and to build communication about the change from the organization to the Change Team and leadership.

Set up hotlines and other ongoing communication processes to deal with rumors, growing concerns, submerged issues, misunderstandings and flare-ups, and act as a conduit to the leadership and Change Team for mid-course corrections.

Another way to assess the different communication and involvement needs is in relation to the degree of commitment that you wish from a group. The more commitment you need, the more involvement they will need in the process of becoming informed.

LEVELS OF INVOLVEMENT

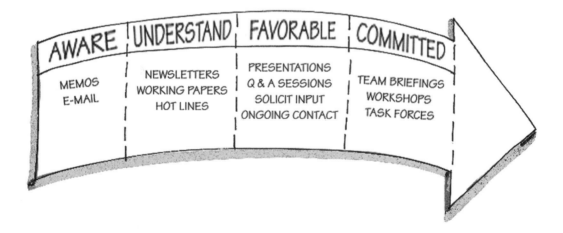

NAVIGATION TOOL:
EMPLOYEE PARTICIPATION WORKSHOP

This workshop is a powerful way to get commitment from people affected by a change. The workshop brings employees together with members of the Change Team to:

- Learn about the proposed change

- Share their reactions, concerns, and ideas

- Design pathways for their ongoing involvement in the change initiative

The workshop is the cornerstone of the two-way communications efforts to stakeholder groups that may also include newsletters, town hall meetings, and videos.

Hold the workshop with as many as 60–250 representatives of the stakeholder groups within a month for their whole team, or as many of them as can attend. The participants act as key conduits of communication to begin the cascade of information through the organization. They also help plan the organization-wide communications effort. This format is used most frequently for the first round of Individual Change Capability Workshops (page 69), relatively early in the design process.

The executive leadership and the Change Team provide leadership to this event. The Change Navigator is the facilitator, with several associates. Bring together managers and participants from the parts of the organization that will be changing, in order to consider the design of the new processes, let go of old baggage, and develop new ways to work together. Both time and money are saved by bringing people together to work out the issues and consider what it will take to make the process operate well.

This type of workshop can also be done with a smaller group, from 6–25 people, representing one (or 2–3 linked) stakeholder groups. This format is usually used later on in the process, and can be repeated for key stakeholder groups at regular intervals, usually every three months. It forms a method for ongoing involvement and growing commitment from that group.

All of the information arising in the workshop should be recorded and a copy of the flip charts and information should be sent to the participants within ten days. Electronic facilitation and recording tools, such as groupware, can be used for recording.

Design for Large-Group Employee Involvement Workshop

■ **Getting Acquainted** (in mixed groups at tables of 6–8)

Structured conversations that quickly bring participants into talking about what they value and find frustrating in their work.

■ **Benchmark Data: Information and Dialogue**

Share what the Change Team is doing, their overall strategic and operational vision.

Participants then discuss what they have heard and have the opportunity to formulate table questions. A dialogue is held about the data in order to convey the gravity of the situation and the magnitude of change needed for long-term viability. Leadership Team members participate in sharing the data and their feelings about it.

This is a key activity in the session: even though the "answers" are not ready, most people appreciate receiving full information about the situation they are in. If they have the opportunity to think it through, they can better contribute to solutions and will be more ready to accept unpleasant alternatives as necessary.

■ **Design Alternatives**

At this point the Change Team either shares the draft design or 2–3 design alternatives. The value of using the second approach is that the Change Team can draw on the thinking of a larger cross-section of the organization. In addition, people throughout the organization will be more personally committed to implementation because they will have been involved in creating the design.

The mixed-table groups will develop table questions to the Change Team about the design, to ensure complete understanding. After the suggestions are grouped by issues or themes, the participants will vote on the most important.

■ **Old Norms and New Principles**

Table groups develop lists of the current organizational norms ("how things get done around here") and share them with the large room. They are grouped into categories. Then tables each work on 1–2 categories, brainstorming lists of new norms or work principles that would make it possible for the new design to work and produce excellent results.

These are shared in the large room. If there will not be large layoffs and it is possible for participants to know roughly what work groups they will be in after the change, then it is best to spend time in the work groups, looking at "What do we still need to find out?" and "What do we need to do differently, if this change is to be successful?" This is a key activity, but needs to be handled creatively if it is known that a large percentage of the group will not be in the company after the change.

Then, each person is asked to consider what this will mean for them personally, using simple written questions, or else 2–3 person groups within the same mixed groups.

■ How Do We Want to be Involved?

People get into table groups now representing their work groups or functions, and brainstorm some of the information they need, and how they want to be involved in the design process. Each team reports to the whole group.

■ New Steps

The whole group now talks about processes for continuing involvement.

Aligning systems with new processes is detailed in Task 4.

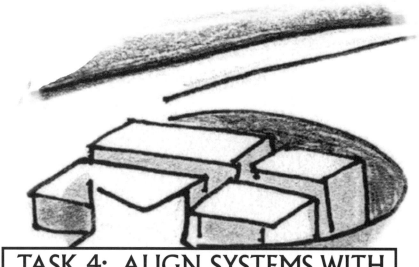

TASK 4: ALIGN SYSTEMS WITH NEW PROCESSES

Key Activities

 ■ *Create Workforce Transition Strategy*

 ■ *Define New Work Contract*

 ■ *Support Employee Growth and Development*

 ■ *Define Human Resoures System Implications for Change*

SETTING THE COURSE

Major changes are very often created by people who are close to operations which then need to be linked directly to the human resource policies and practices, that recruit, select, train, supervise, assess, reward and develop employees for the organization. These policies operationalize how the organization works, and they need to reflect some of the new thinking about working in teams, working across boundaries, new interpersonal skills, continual learning and development, and rewarding people for results.

Change must be anchored in an organization's DNA, its core policies, processes, structures and values about how people are brought in, treated and rewarded. Any major change will involve deep changes in how people work; these must be aligned with changes in how each of the organization's human policies fit with the change.

While human resources people are part of many change efforts, and the Change Navigator is frequently part of human resources, the overall redesign of these policies is complex. Yet, if they are not changed, employees are apt to find themselves being asked to do one set of things, while being rewarded, selected and held accountable for others. Or, practices in one area—such as reward and compensation, do not fit with those in other areas—such as supervision. For change to "take" in an organization, its policies around people need to be aligned with them. People's behavior will usually flow toward what is rewarded and measured, rather than what is stated.

Human resources policies also reflect the ways that the organization values and supports its people. If change is needed, but people are pushed to change through threat and intimidation, they will go along, but the outcome will be compliance not commitment. People will feel so disrupted and stressed out by the change that they will withdraw at the very time the organization most needs their involvement.

Core Activities

Outcomes

■ Communicate about, define, and carry out the transition of people out of the organization and/or into new jobs

■ Redesign organizational policies, practices, and structures to support the new organizational values and behaviors

■ The organization provides transition processes that result in commitment to seeing the transition through from those that stay

■ Every employee develops self and career-management skills

■ Clarity about how the human resources system is linked to the success of the change-management intiative

■ Changes are reeinforced by selection, reward, performance management, and development policies

CHALLENGES

Change Means Some Job Loss and Transition

When an organization considers change, the first question everybody has is "What will happen to me?" Until they have some grounding in what to expect, how their future is involved, even if there is no definitive commitment, they will not have much real energy to be involved in change. Executives too often respond to the uncertainty of the early phases of change by saying "We don't know what will happen." This may be somewhat true, but people feel that some parameters have been set—perhaps cost-cutting goals, or needs for increased efficiency, that give them some sense of where their futures lie.

Providing people with some sort of security, perhaps by simply telling people what everybody can expect from the organization during the change, demonstrates respect for the people and, what employees need to hear before they can commit to a new, more demanding and complex organization.

Some executives have difficulty acknowledging and dealing with the emotional reality of impending job loss. Some people will lose jobs, some stay, and some will leave the organization voluntarily. Reinforcing the dignity of people through the process pushes up against desires for speed, planning, security and control. Poorly conceived and carried out workforce transitions can permanently impair the motivation of the people left in the company, and lead to unwanted defections and transitions.

Catalyze Change

Employee behavior follows what is rewarded and expected, not what is asked for. Human resources policies can act as a force to resist and undermine new initiatives, if the organization has a deeply entrenched and vested interest in a traditional human resources bureaucracy. Focus on the structure of the human resource policies to actively catalyze change. Encourage flexibility to experiment with new initiatives, especially if the changes are focused on a regional or divisional level.

GUIDING PRINCIPLES

■ *The values displayed throughout the process will strongly influence the success of the program.* Employees do not dissociate their feelings from their job. How you treat them determines how they treat the customer and impacts how they work. Leadership and organizational credibility and trust, the most important factors in a high-performance company, are gravely strained during major change. If they aren't attended to, the company will have difficulty recovering.

■ *Preserving people's dignity is the most important focus of successful change.* If those who stay have their dignity removed, they will not perform well for the organization in the medium- or long-term. If people are forced to leave without dignity, those who remain will resent the leadership and the organization. The way people leave affects the people who stay. Before major changes have a complete plan in place to deal with all the transitions that will be needed. When people lose their jobs there is an impact on their families as well as the community at large.

■ *Achieving successful transition involves saying good-bye before you say hello.* Transitions are a way of providing closure and new beginnings for people who stay in the organization. In order to let go of old ways, patterns and processes, people often need to say good-bye. Those who stay need to begin anew. Good good-byes make good hellos.

■ *Employees need help to understand they are working under an evolving work contract.* The set of expectations and responsibilities that are implicitly expected between the organization and employees has shifted with the advent of continual change. The workplace can no longer guarantee employment, or regular promotions. Competitive demands make this impossible to offer, as it had in the past. Employees are increasingly motivated by different factors: involvement, meaningful work, opportunities for self-development and learning. The organization needs employees who adopt a different role and a broader set of responsibilities. The company must renegotiate its web of expectations, obligations and mutual responsibilities with employees. This new contract is the foundation for the new human resources policies. The design process begins with the values, behaviors, competencies and attitudes that you want in the workplace, and then designs processes to fit them.

■ ***People need to learn the skills of taking responsibility for their own careers.*** The new workplace requires individuals who can be self-starting and able to identify their own development needs and potential. Gaining maximum benefit from the change initiative will be dependent on the extent to which individuals internalize and adopt this change.

■ ***Use human resources processes to drive and support the change.*** Human resources is a strategic element critical to the success of change efforts, not an afterthought or option. Change cannot be sustained unless it becomes part of the policies, procedures and infrastructure of the workplace. In order to sustain a change process, the ways that people are recruited, trained, supervised, evaluated and developed, must be shifted to reflect the new competencies, qualities and attitudes desired. People will tend to behave according to how they are measured and rewarded. Human resources policies are among the most traditional elements of the organization, and they must be aggressively modified.

■ ***View human resources processes as a whole, not as separate parts to be altered individually.*** In the new workplace, human resources policies cannot be considered and designed in isolation, but must be approached as an integrated into the change process. Processes for selecting, motivating, rewarding and managing people should be designed by human resources staff in partnership with the people who are regulated by the policies as well as the managers who must implement them. Use human resources and break down barriers and distinctions between human resources functions, and between human resources and managers and team leaders.

KEY ACTIVITIES FOR TASK 4

ACTIVITY 1: Create Workforce Transition Strategy

This activity should be done as soon as possible, because employees cannot be engaged in the design process and considering the organization's future, until they understand the parameters for their own personal future. If possible, the major guiding values and principles should be presented at the Individual Change Capability Workshop.

Determine values around the transition process. Underlying all workforce reductions and changes is a set of values about people and their worth to the organization. If people are to be involved in changing the organization, they need to know when, how, and under what conditions they will be asked to leave, or expectations for learning new skills and taking up new jobs. These include both policies and values. They need to be announced before the change process begins, so people can pursue their own development and opportunities. Employees want to know how they can demonstrate their value to the organization, and what is expected of employees who wish to stay. Assess learnings from past experiences: do again, don't do again.

Define and present layoff package:

- Early out—early retirement

- Outplacement services—choice points, options

- Legal issues

- Employee assistance services

- Working with unions

The organization needs to be aware that they want key employees to stay, not leave. The package must be fair and acceptable, but efforts must be made to retain key employees. Too often, the most adaptable and creative employees are the first to seek other opportunities, leaving the timid, the confused, the indecisive, and the less competent to stay.

For maximum retention focus on the following two factors. Create processes that clarify how this will be done.

- The organization, through the change design process, will decide what skills it needs in its employees

- Employees themselves will have to decide whether they have them or if they want to develop them

The following model is useful:

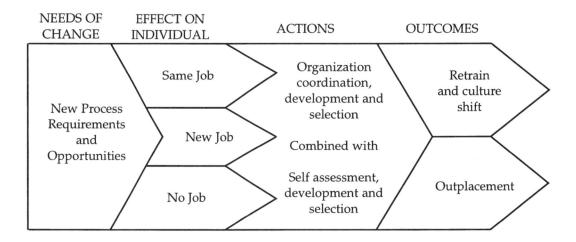

NEEDS OF CHANGE	EFFECT ON INDIVIDUAL	ACTIONS	OUTCOMES
New Process Requirements and Opportunities	Same Job	Organization coordination, development and selection	Retrain and culture shift
	New Job	Combined with	
	No Job	Self assessment, development and selection	Outplacement

Design the process for employee involvement in job transition. This should be a sub-council of the Change Team, and consist not just of human resources professionals, but representatives of key employee groups affected, unions and various levels of the organization. They should monitor the way policies are applied and be available to respond to concerns, and conflicts, and to monitor feelings about the transition policies.

Design an ongoing communication plan for two-way exchange and clarification of employee job futures, including hotlines, newsletters, video conferences, large- and small-group meetings, e-mail, job center and learning opportunities. Tell the truth, fully, and be sure to include specifics, such as dates, numbers, and other clear information to help guide choices.

ACTIVITY 2: Define New Work Contract

Explore New Values, Vision and Workplace Expectations

Assemble a Human Resources Redesign Team consisting of human resources staff and line managers experienced and sensitive to the human side of change.

Begin by looking at the proposed change, and how the workplace is, and needs to evolve.

Define the expectations and shape of the new workplace, the new values about work performance and human resources, and how employee behavior will have to change in terms of attitude, scope of responsibilities and behavior:

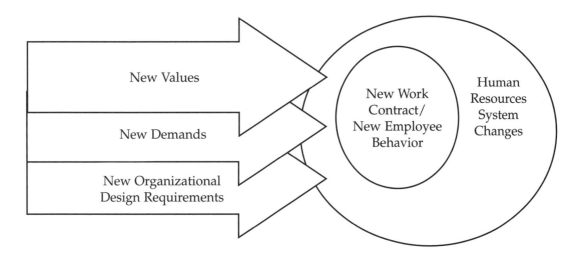

Define New Work Contract and Expectations

The Human Resources Redesign Team drafts a New Work Contract defining the new expectations and proposed values that will become part of the organization.

The contract will help guide the process of:

- Identifying the new work roles and key behaviors that will enable individuals to be successful in the new workplace

- Committing resources (time, space, staff, money) to enable employees to be exposed to, acquire and master these new skills

- Providing a coherent developmental process for skill development setting new expectations for career development

This statement will be circulated to the top leadership, Change Team, the Employee Involvement Council and various elements of the organization, for discussion and feedback. After brief but extensive exploration, the contract will be finalized and shared.

ACTIVITY 3: Support Employee Growth and Development

Conduct Personal and Career Self-Assessment

A Self-Assessment Process helps individuals assess their willingness and ability to work well in the new culture. This assessment will help individuals see where they stand in relation to what is needed to create a new workplace and offers some resources for skill development. This will enable people to make the choice whether to go or stay, and if they decide to stay, have them take responsibility for the new learning they need.

Create Internal Redeployment Process

Create an internal redeployment plan, with clear parameters for what new jobs will be available, when, how employees can begin to develop their capacity to take them, how decisions will be made, priorities, preferences, and where to go for further information. There should be a clear internal reapplication process for seeking, qualifying and taking on new jobs as the organization moves to implement major changes.

Set up a career center where people can go for information, counseling, and to seek learning opportunities.

Develop Realignment/Recruitment Plan

- Design realignment orientation to new culture

- Understand how to control the early outs

- Develop plan to retain key people

Develop a Training Plan for New Competencies

As the new workplace and design is created, the specific needs, competencies and new skills that the organization needs must be defined. Since knowledge is a critical resource, the emphasis should always be on internal training and development, rather than outside recruiting of new skills.

The following issues must be considered:

- What capabilities will be needed?

- What is the current set of competencies?

- What core competencies need to be developed?

- What training can develop internal candidates?

ACTIVITY 4: Define Human Resources System Implications of Change

The Human Resources Redesign Team will look at the implications of change on the following human resources processes:

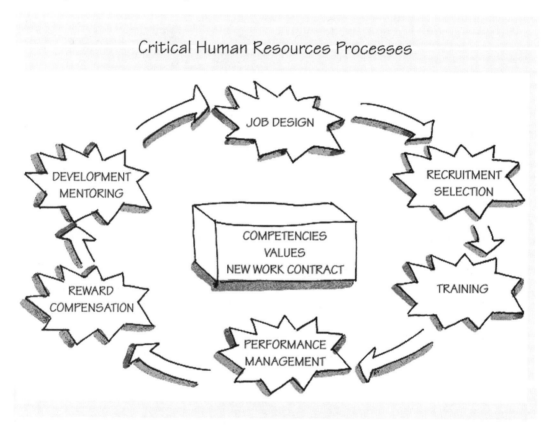

The above graphic places the various aspect of human resources onto a developmental process, which looks at the cycle of design entry, learning, support, assessment and development that makes up human resources development. By looking at it within this format, clients can look at common goals, and combine the various aspects of their strategy into an integrated whole.

Redesign Human Resources Systems and Policies

The Human Resources Redesign Team representing the diversity of the organization, will assess the current and desired human resources strategic processes and structures, focusing on the work values they support, and how they fit with each other. Some of the areas they will focus on are:

- Define key areas where the systems do not support the emerging values, organizational needs, new competencies and the processes that need to change most.

- Look at new values and propose strategies for overcoming gaps through policies and processes. Define key areas to initiate an overall strategy for phasing in of human resources innovation and change.

- Undertake a rethinking of its approach to human resources, starting from the new demands, values, expectations and change design requirements that are evolving in the organization.

- Design systems that center on the general qualities needed in employees, a process for developing the specific new skills needed by employees who work in the redesigned processes.

- Create a model department—look at how the people processes operate. Make sure it functions as it should.

- Train and support managers to utilize new human resources processes.

Wave Three examines methods for sustaining transformations.

Wave Three

SUSTAINING THE TRANSFORMATION

Key Tasks

- *Champion New Ways*
- *Cascade Change Leadership*
- *Develop New Teams*
- *Anchor Organizational Learning*

WAVE THREE: INTRODUCTION

Wave Three is the implementation of a collaborative design throughout the organization. It is about changing behavior as well as changing deeper attitudes, ways of doing things, and most important, each person learning and taking up a new role and set of responsibilities within the organization.

Traditionally, implementation is considered an afterthought, a mundane project management task of scheduling hundreds of little tasks, deploying resources such as people, offering training and setting change in motion. The reality is quite different—even if the planning is elegant, clear and persuasive. People find it far more difficult to really change. Things do not turn out as planned, and the actual effects of new behavior are quite different from what were predicted. Implementation often turns first into chaos, then confusion, then apathy, as the original plans are frantically scaled down and projections are reduced.

The difficulty is that the real challenge of change is not creating good plans, but creating plans that people understand clearly, are committed to, and can actually do. Taking the time and providing the resources and care to put them into effect can be difficult. The art of implementation can almost be considered another round of collaborative design—with as much care, thought, communication, uncertainty, and struggle as the design phase. In effect, each wave of planned change goes over much the same ground, with deeper and more consequential change taking place. The processes of Waves One and Two are repeated once more, with leaders getting involved, the Change Team activating numerous groups and teams, and communicating the effects.

The major element of Wave Three is continuing what has been done—not disbanding the various design groups, but instead shifting them to implementing the designs they have created.

The following pages show how we must champion new ways, cascade change leadership, develop new teams, and learn to anchor organizational learning.

TASK 1: CHAMPION NEW WAYS

Key Activities

■ *Recharter Change Implementation Team*

■ *Support Change Through Leader Actions*

■ *Support Renewal During Implementation*

■ *Align Activities of All Integration Processes*

■ *Hold Reviews of the Change Implementation*

SETTING THE COURSE

Leaders—sponsors, top executives, and the Change Leader—really come into their own in this phase. Instead of sitting back and watching things come about, the Leadership Team is deeply engaged in several levels of change. First, they are engaged in their own implementation of a new leadership design. Second, they are themselves learning new skills and habits. And third, if people become tired, drained, frustrated, and upset yet again, the leaders must be there to cheerlead, reward, renew, and sustain the effort. They must also be ready for new external crises, as well as implementation crises caused by unintended effects of proposed change. As the changes become real, people need tremendous support. And, as the results come in, people need appropriate rewards, not just a trophy or testimonial at a retreat.

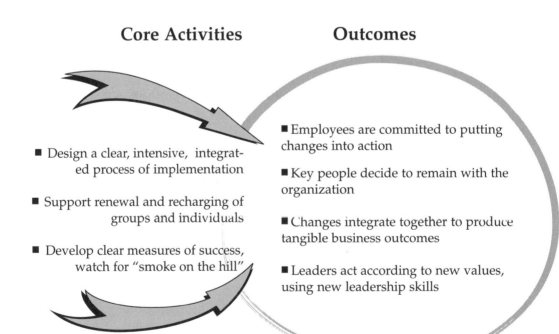

Core Activities

- Design a clear, intensive, integrated process of implementation

- Support renewal and recharging of groups and individuals

- Develop clear measures of success, watch for "smoke on the hill"

Outcomes

- Employees are committed to putting changes into action

- Key people decide to remain with the organization

- Changes integrate together to produce tangible business outcomes

- Leaders act according to new values, using new leadership skills

CHALLENGES

Promoting Capability as Well as Change

As the organization shifts from design to implementation, the change initiative requires action. Each person must do more than change behavior, the whole organization (or group that is changing) must adopt new values and a new style of doing work. For change to "stick," groups of people throughout the organization need to do new things in coordination with others whom they are not accustomed to working with. None of this happens on its own, without capable leadership.

Loss of Talent

At the time of implementation there are many changes of personnel—especially losses. Not only those who were asked to leave, but often people who are talented, who have learned new marketable skills, or who just become frustrated or tired of the process, elect to leave. There can be a brain drain if leaders are not prepared to prevent it. New leaders who have grown through the design process may feel there is no place for them in the new organization. They don't want to return to their old jobs, even if they are redesigned, and they find the pathways to new responsibility are not clear. New leaders may feel that they have not been supported, rewarded, or respected enough in the change, and they do not feel they can continue to fight for new ways if the organization is pulling back. Only the Leadership Team can deal with these high-level dilemmas.

The Need for Renewal

It is not enough to change, the organization must continue to change. Leadership must lead a process of renewal after the stress, disruption, and pain of major change. The organization is wounded, and it is important that leadership recognize this and lead people through a process of recommitting to the organization's new future. The executives can show by their actions that they value learning in addition to more traditional performance measures. People need time to rest, and opportunities to renew themselves. That does not mean they stop work, but rather that they have opportunities to grow, develop, and use what they have learned.

It is important to maintain momentum and keep the interest alive. Many leaders might begin to feel exhausted from the effort. Initial excitement for change can give way to skepticism and disappointment. The challenge is to guide the organization through the hardest part of the change process—implementation.

Crises Amid Change

Change outside the organization continues. Few changes, especially those that take time, can proceed without the organization encountering an unexpected crisis. The challenge is for the leadership to incorporate the crisis into the change process, not reject or postpone change. Employees are alert to the slightest sign that the change process is not supported, and the vitality of fighting fires and overcoming crisis can lead implementers to abandon their processes and slip back to old ways, albeit inadvertently.

GUIDING PRINCIPLES

■ *Support the people you want to keep.* Reward the heroes; take time with the most important people. Make sure the people who are real leaders, who are willing to change, are part of important work in implementation. It is especially important, after you have asked other people to leave, not to quickly go outside the organization for new talent. As you bring in new talent, you provoke an exit of people who feel undermined or pushed aside. Also, leaders need to be alert to internal opposition, and take firm steps not to support or avoid it. Change is a delicate process; it is not irreversible. If the change starts off with lots of excitement, but then the people in the center lose their burning desire, the change will begin to falter, and eventually reverse itself, to return to old ways.

■ *You are the first team to implement change.* The changes in organizational design, structure, work processes, and expectations begin at the top. That means that the Executive Team has to change radically in order to support a new organization. At the implementation phase, the Executive Team has to visibly and openly engage in its own change process. Executives need to learn new skills, assess each other, and deliver real value to the organization. The Leadership Team needs its own Change Navigator, most often an external senior consultant, who has the authority and credibility to coach and confront the top team.

■ *Use the symbolic power of the executive position.* Provide inspiration—remain in touch with the actual state of people's energy—ensure there are processes in place through management and human resources to minimize "survivor sickness" or the demoralization and burnout that result from most long processes of complex change.

Use highly visible gestures to show personal commitment to change: such as promotions, large meetings and public interviews. Give up symbols that remind people of the old ways: a parking space next to the door, or the executive dining room. Create new symbols that convey the new ways.

■ *At different points in the process you will need to be "hands-on" and "hands-off."* Early on—be hands on. Set clear and challenging goals, focusing efforts on delivering those goals, and being unyielding in applying resources, time, and attention throughout the organization. Later on—be hands off. Once you gain buy-in from a critical mass of people, it is important that the Change Team and key stakeholders spread responsibility for the change effort widely, and the decision-making power that goes with it.

- ■ ***Be alert to signs of bad news and potential difficulty.*** The pressure is on everyone in the organization to produce. This leads to an environment where people can cut corners, avoid dealing with difficulties, and keep bad news from the top. Part of change capability is creating a change process where people are not reluctant to bring bad news to the top. This can be said over and over again, but the reward structure, pressures from external constituencies and from the organization as a whole, tends to press for closure. It takes a lot of energy to maintain the openness to change. The Leadership Team has to be active in setting the example of willingness to see real problems. Work with leadership and the implementation team to prevent an upsurge in turf politics.

- ■ ***Keep information flowing both up and down.*** The dilemma is that people want to be rewarded for results, and bad news is usually about lack of results. So people can expect to be blamed for not getting results. There is no easy cure for this paradox.

Leaders, however, have to be alert to the tendency for people to want to deliver good news and not look at problems. If change leaders do not have the trust to bring issues up as they arise, and to address complications and mid-course changes, the implementation will run aground. Nothing proceeds as planned, and every implementation process contains an unexpected change or crisis which tests the mettle and the flexibility of the Change Leaders.

KEY ACTIVITIES FOR TASK 1

ACTIVITY 1: Recharter Change Implementation Team for the New Task

The Change Team evolves into a new role in Wave Three. Too often, just as implementation begins, the members of the Change Team feel that their work is done, or become burned out from their labors. In addition, implementation demands new skills of teaching, coaching, and letting go. The Leadership Team needs to recharter the Change Team, refining it as the Change Implementation Team. The leaders should look closely at each member of the team, recruiting some new members, and allowing other members to move on. However, if too many people leave the team, continuity and a sense of history may be lost.

Ensure that a Change Implementation Team leader is in place who shares the values and beliefs of the Change Leader. Many change processes falter because the implementation is led by someone who is an excellent action-oriented implementer, but does not share the deeper motivations of those who launched the change.

ACTIVITY 2: Support Change Through Leader Actions

Use all available means to demonstrate continued commitment to realizing the change. Acknowledge that it has been difficult and will remain so. Visibly support the future ways of working, through:

- Attention to who is promoted and given special assignments

- Behavior in meetings, communication processes

- One-to-one coaching for direct reports needs to focus on behavior as well as business results

- Continued balance of active leadership and listening

Arrange for the leadership to receive feedback periodically from the Change Team on how the Leadership Team is doing in leading the change effort. Use either a few simple written, open-ended questions in a quantitative questionnaire designed around assessing key leadership behaviors, or Change Navigator interviews.

Celebrate successes: with them, and to the broader organization about their work.

Give new values and work processes teeth by asking them to be clarified, made specific, and supporting them through reward systems and through your own example. A gathering about new organizational values or expectations with key participants representing different work groups is the kind of activity that supports implementations.

ACTIVITY 3: Support Renewal During Implementation

The organization has asked for tremendous energy, time and commitment from its employees, especially those who are Change Leaders. Just as implementation begins, people may feel overwhelmingly tired.

The top leader has to create processes for people to renew themselves, and teams must do the same. Renewal includes:

- The importance of organizational vitality

- Developing a shared approach to recognizing vitality

- The difference between elegant processes and a vital organization

- Identifying what kills vitality and remove obstacles

- Ensuring that the organization values learning, as well as performance

Renewal activities are necessary to sustain performance. They include rotating people into new jobs and new areas of work, offering opportunities to learn and grow, helping people to support and reward each other for good work, and defining midpoint successes that have clear rewards.

ACTIVITY 4: Align Activities of All Integration Processes

In order to ensure ongoing connectedness with the Change Implementation Team, clearly articulate expectations for them.

Drop in on Change Implementation Team meetings informally, and listen—participate occasionally, without overwhelming them.

Visibly demonstrate support for the Change Team to the broader organization, and be available, to allow the Change Team to ask for what it needs.

Ensure that the communication and employee-involvement process continues as implementation begins.

Be sure that there is a clear master plan for implementation that everyone is aware of. This plan should be flexible, but contain clear commitments and expectations of concrete changes and their expected effects.

Be sure there are clear measures and milestones for implementation, and that there is good data collection so that real problems can be flagged and dealt with.

ACTIVITY 5: Hold Reviews of the Change Implementation

Conduct a feedback/assessment process on the effectiveness of the communication about the change to ensure that the leadership has accurate information so it does not form an illusory picture of where the organization is. This process helps to start a dialogue with the organization about the proposed change and expectations.

Because the leadership is so committed to the change and has already thought through the issues, they often assume that there are fewer problems than people experience "down in the ranks." The Change Navigator can play a useful role in helping to establish processes that will give the leaders personal experiences of where people actually are:

- Pace of change
- Attitudes toward change
- Level of motivation
- Beliefs about the organization's and leadership's motivation

Check that original assumptions are still valid.

Check the continuing fit of the original assumptions with the current business situation and implementation plan.

Passing on skills and processes are explored in Task 2.

TASK 2: CASCADE CHANGE LEADERSHIP

Key Activities

 ■ *Provide New Skills for Managers to Lead Change: Leading Change Workshop*

 ■ *Coach and Support Managers to Take Up New Rules*

SETTING THE COURSE

Change Leadership is not a temporary set of activities for a temporary group of Change Leaders who then fade into the woodwork. The skills and processes used by the Change Team have to be passed on to each of the managers and leaders in the changing organization. Each manager has to learn and take on a new expanded role in the new workplace. This task involves processes to teach and transfer these new leadership skills throughout the organization. The new organization needs many leaders, not just a few. In fact, to some degree almost everyone needs to become a Change Leader. The skill and capability transfer process is implemented with these activities.

Core Activities

- Successfully transfer leadership of change from the Change Teams to the managers responsible for completing implementation

- Change Leadership skills are learned and applied to implementation

Outcomes

- Managers learn the skills of becoming leaders, not managers of change

- All managers know their roles and responsibilities in expediting the initiatives

- Transfer of ownership to implementation leaders is completed

CHALLENGES

Share Ownership of the New Organization

Choose the right people for implementation responsibility. Membership and owner-ship issues need to be dealt with. It is important to choose the right people, take actions that will maintain the spirit and integrity of the guiding vision, and be willing to integrate new ideas from new members.

People Revert to Old Ways When Under Pressure

Managers in new leadership roles may revert to old management behaviors under pressure for results during change. The process of changing involves both rational and emotional learning, trying out new behaviors and practicing them, and under-standing how they will be useful. You cannot simply legislate new behavior, you need to teach, support, and reinforce the new behaviors.

Changes Are Not Complete Until They Get Results

As many make changes, results can get neglected. People underestimate the time, energy, and resources needed to expedite the change, and overestimate the results. The Change Team must adopt realistic expectations and assess the degree to which they are achieved.

Change Dims the More Distant You Get from the Designers

The Change Team and the top leaders know what is needed to change. The other Change Teams and various stakeholders know somewhat less. Employees who have to change often know the least about the change. The skills that the Change Leaders take for granted now have to be replicated throughout the organization. People need to learn new skills before they can really change. Otherwise they are just going through the motions.

GUIDING PRINCIPLES

- **Educate and develop new skills in people before delegating.** Most people involved in the change process have never been part of a change effort of that magnitude. They will need to be educated before they can contribute. They have to "know how" as well as "want to."

- **Implementing new work processes is a major change for line managers.** Moving the processes from design to implementation will involve bringing in a large number of new line managers. They have to help their people work in new ways and will require new skills to help them manage this change. For some it will be completely new. The Change Team who will be very familiar with the concepts by this stage must not lose sight of this, and must think things through from the line managers' perspective.

- **Acknowledge people's resentments and losses arising from the change process.** Change creates winners and losers. The psychological contract they have with the organization has changed. Many of the key stakeholders may be feeling a sense of loss, and will fight the change. Acknowledge the potential and real losses that people will feel and deal with them directly at the emotional level. Allow people to express their fears, sense of loss, and concerns, and include them in the process.

KEY ACTIVITIES FOR TASK 2

ACTIVITY 1: Provide New Skills for Managers to Lead Change: Leading Change Workshop

Design a clear implementation strategy outlining where and how change in manager/ leader behavior needs to occur.

If the change is a reengineering effort, bringing in the team who will lead the new effort needs to happen sooner rather than later. Typically many changes represent key features of the new organization. A task force can take the lead in creating these new features.

Teach Change Leaders the fundamental principles of redesigning organizations and teams, guiding them through the key decisions, and help them define an effective process for staffing the new organization.

Explain and clarify the structure of the new organization. People will be concerned about the new structure, and particularly, where they fit in. The Change Team needs to address the questions of:

- What the new organization looks like from a structural point of view

- Will teams be the primary unit for the new organization?

- What do the teams look like in the new organization?

- Will managers be facilitators?

- Who will the new leaders be?

Determine who needs to deal with what part of the change process. Select key process owners of the new organization. It is particularly important here that the new leaders adopt the new performance management process as well as other new human resources policies. If they are not committed to the new approach, they and the change are likely to fail.

The Change Implementation Team needs to take responsibility for identifying and choosing key players/process owners for new roles in the new organization. It is important to ensure that politics do not get in the way. People in the client system will posture for position and there will likely be a number of issues that arise in the process that will be uncomfortable to discuss.

The change process continues while new leaders are chosen. Too often, during the implementation phase, leaders of the change process or Change Teams delegate the implementation too far downward and momentum is lost.

Clarify purpose, role, outcomes, deliverables, milestones, and measures of each key activity going forward.

Clarify the role of the Change Implementation Team. Some Change Teams dissolve once the change effort is complete. If this is the case, then Change Team members need to be prepared for this and find new roles for themselves. Others continue in different forms, particularly for those change efforts that take years to produce significant and enduring results.

Implement and measure the effects of the changes. The Change Implementation Team will be responsible for implementing and measuring success. Others throughout the organization will be playing key roles in the implementation: the Change Team oversees the process—ensuring that the plans are applied, helping work through difficult issues, and revising plans as needed.

NAVIGATION TOOL:
LEADING CHANGE WORKSHOP

Managers have the greatest amount of learning and change to achieve success at a change. Before a team can change, the managers/leaders of the team have to be introduced to the new expectations and behaviors of change leadership.

Managers should have begun to learn the new ways. This is a template for a two-day workshop to teach managers the new rules for change leadership. The workshop uses a model of five lenses, five key perspectives on the organization that an effective Change Leader must learn. It goes over the key activities and skills the leader must demonstrate in each of these five lenses, or perspectives.*

The Need for Leadership of Change

The purpose of this work session is to focus on your role in leading others through change using tools taken from the five lenses to produce business results and build the capability for future change.

Without Change Leadership, Change Efforts Will Fail

In the past decade, while every organization wanted to change, the vast majority of attempts at major change were doomed to fail. They fail not because of the intention, but because of faulty implementation. Just because an organization has decided it has to change does not mean that it will be successful.

In an American Management Association study of 259 top executives in 1993, many felt unsuccessful in managing change. The biggest reasons why change-management efforts fail are:

- Insufficient attention to the change
- No formal change program
- Lack of expertise at changing

Change is not a linear or technical process. It cannot be placed into neat and easy categories.

* Leading Change Workshops are available through Changeworks, Inc., 461 Second St., #232, San Francisco, CA 94107, (415) 546-4488. www.cworksinc.com

A Harvard University study of leaders of change in organizations found that for:

76%	Implementing the change took far longer than expected
74%	Problems surfaced that had not been identified
66%	Coordination is not effective
64%	Competing activities and crises distracted from the change

To succeed at implementing change everyone has to be on board and work for it. This workshop looks at how you can become a Change Leader at implementing the strategic change that your company desires.

Setting the Context for Change Leadership

We are in an unprecedented period of change. Even the character of change is changing. Never before have the factors of magnitude, momentum, and complexity converged to influence the impact change is having on our lives, our work, and our world.

Talk about the need to lead change is the challenge of today for every organization. All living systems grow and develop according to an S curve. Inevitably, after fast growth, any organization reaches limits to growth and must find a way to renew itself.

What is your view of where your company is right now on the S curve?

At some point in change, a second wave of change begins, sometimes at the height of the first wave of success. An organization can begin a new curve while they still continue to operate on the old one. The more quickly they start up the new curve, the more successful they will be at anticipating change, rather than reacting to it. But this new curve is also a source of tension, as people have to pursue two sometimes conflicting tasks at once. The challenge is to build on our strengths and expand upon them.

The question is not whether to change, but when to change, how deeply, and how quickly. Organizations that learn to change effectively, appropriately, and quickly will have the sustainable competitive advantage for the future. The cost of change is high, but the more quickly an organization changes, the more ready they will be to compete and thrive.

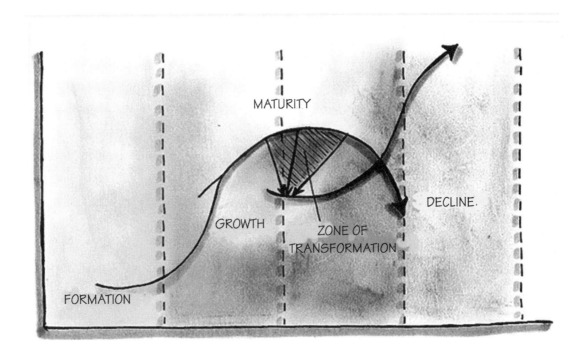

Preparing for a Change

Now we will focus a little more closely on planning for the short-term. Some changes have been made clear to you; others are still to come. However, you can make some educated guesses about what some of the future changes will be, and even begin to anticipate and work towards them in your team. You are asked to initiate some changes, but you can also anticipate and plan for the next round by preparing your team and yourself.

Taking Your Learning Back to Your Team

You can begin to use what you learn in this workshop when you return to your team. Presumably you will share what you have learned with your team, and even do some of the activities you will experience here with your team together.

The Five Lenses of Change Leadership

Have people recall an organizational change that they experienced in the past, especially remembering the role of the leader of the change. This is a chance for them to hear stories from each other about real Change Leaders.

> ***Ask:***   What worked?
>
> What didn't work?
>
> What did the leader do, specifically, to make it succeed?
>
> How was the role or behavior of the leader different than the traditional manager's role?

Whatever you do, your job has changed in the past decade. Nobody is *just* a manager anymore. Your key task today is to lead a group in an organization that is constantly changing. Being a leader during major change is different from being a traditional manager. In an organization that has to change fast, every manager must learn new skills.

Leading change is a difficult business. Everyone seems to have a different perspective on reality. It takes time and patience to reduce the confusion and reconcile the differences in people's view of reality. To deal effectively with the complexity and uncertainty of change, leaders need to consider actions from five different perspectives.

    I.   **Relationships lens**

   II.   **Culture lens**

  III.   **Structure lens**

  IV.   **Stakeholder lens**

   V.   **Information lens**

Leaders of change are challenged to maintain performance under chaotic conditions. Teams may be confused, resistant, and disheartened. Job security, company loyalty, and career development may no longer be available as rewards for performance. Yet, Change Leaders have to build and maintain a motivated and productive workforce under these conditions.

Discuss the role of Change Leader and how this differs from traditional management.

Introduction to Lenses and Tools

Let's say you are having trouble with your distance vision. You find yourself squinting to bring the distance into view. You get headaches. So, you go to an expert who uses a system of overlapping lenses to diagnose your problem. The expert selects a combination of lenses to create a unique prescription that will align and balance your eyesight and enhance the quality, depth, range and clarity of your vision.

During change you may have similar problems. Faced with confusion, pressure, and ambiguity, you may try even harder to do what you have always done. You put the old habitual solution on the new problems, even though they don't always fit. You apply simple solutions to complex problems because you are pressured from all sides. You are "blind" to other ways.

Changing workplaces are alive with stories about what is happening and what should be happening. Partial truths, information silos and crisis mentality keep managers fighting operational fires instead of responding to the complexities of the changing organization. It is common for organizations to propose one-way, overly simplistic solutions to complex problems.

Complex Problems/Multiple Solutions

Today's problems defy a simple solution. Leaders need multiple perspectives to succeed. You need to understand that any event or process can serve or thwart change. Effective leaders use multiple lenses to decide which issues are likely to be relevant and which are likely to be effective in any given situation.

Leaders have to take on many tasks to lead change effectively. They have to do more than tell people what to do and have them comply. In change, they need to help people rethink how they work and what they do, while still producing continual results.

Leaders tend to have one or two things that they do to get results. In times of change, the leader needs to expand his or her repertoire.

To help this, we have designed a model that looks at five lenses. A lens is a way of looking at what is important about change that leads to specific actions, what we call levers for change. Each lens points to one or more key leverage points by which a Change Leader can help create change.

Each lens represents a central theme, focus, or perspective on organizational events. A lens represents a way of thinking about or looking at some part of the organizational system. Looking at the organization through all five lenses helps leaders get a big picture, multi-dimensional view so that they can create a coherent plan for sustainable change.

Skills and Tools for Each Lens

In the workshop, you will learn to use tools from each of the five lenses:

- Use the **Relationship** lens to effectively announce a change, deal with resistance, and encourage communication that identifies issues and resolves differences.

   —Announce a change to your team

   —Overcome individuals' resistance to a change

- Use the **Culture** lens to create a roadmap for change and offer a direction they can believe in.

    —Look at drivers of change in the environment

    —Create a shared team vision (building on a corporate vision)

    —Identify cultural obstacles to the change

- Use the **Structure** lens to clarify and realign goals, roles, responsibilities, authority, and decision making to support the change effort.

    —Look at how to add value to your customers

    —Identify opportunities to move authority and decision making down

- Use the **Stakeholder** lens to align agendas and balance interests to reduce concerns and conflict, and build coalitions among those who have a stake in achieving results.

    —Design activities for ongoing stakeholder involvement

    —Create agreement with your Sponsor for support to change

- Use the **Information** lens to locate and provide reliable data and feedback to measure and improve performance.

    —Design process metrics that support and reinforce the change

At the end of the workshop you will be able to use all five lenses with your team as tools for realigning change goals and addressing change implementation issues.

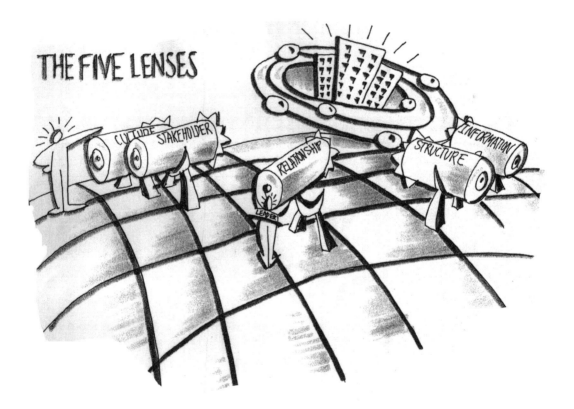

I. Relationship Lens: From Resistance to Commitment

The relationship lens focuses on leadership through building collaborative relationships with the team, understanding their responses to change, and supporting them to change.

The Relationship Leader will use insights from the denial and resistance phases of the transition curve to lead the team into exploration and commitment.

The general method for leading using relationship involves developing collaborative leadership, getting team members involved in designing and implementing change.

You cannot keep yourself or your team from moving through each phase of transition. Yet some people and some teams move more quickly, and more effectively, through the phases. You can influence:

- How *long* it takes you and your team to move through the phases

- How *deeply* the change effects you or your team (how deep the curve is)

Helping your team move through each phase of transition demands different skills of leadership. What works at one phase can be useless if most team members are in another phase. There are specific key skills of leadership to lead your team through each phase of transition.

Different Parts of the Organization Move Through Change at Different Rates

Different parts of the organization can go through transition at different rates and at different times. Talk about how the top of the organization learns about a change first, and has more time to move through denial.

One response to change is characterized by a desire of leaders to see their teams instantly swing over the chasm of change. Moving from commitment to the old way immediately to commitment to the new way is called the **Tarzan Swing.**

Some people expect you to just get over your feelings, step out of them, and put them aside. A very few people are really able to do this, while many others think they can and instead hide their feelings and the effects of change from others, and even from themselves.

Sometimes it can seem like someone has done the Tarzan Swing because you didn't see or hear about their process through the other phases. Sometimes it looks like managers moved immediately into commitment because they are hiding their feelings, or because they heard about the change earlier and had a chance to move through the phases before announcing the change to you.

You may feel pressure from some parts of the organization to move immediately to commitment. Remember that each phase of the change process contributes to your ability to commit to and successfully implement change. Let yourself experience all four stages, just be sure to keep yourself moving and not get stuck in any one phase. Ignoring the feelings of any one stage may just mean that you have to come back later and complete the work of the stage.

Change Meetings as a Tool of Relationship Leaders

When you are dealing with change, you need the most complete and timely information from your team, and you need their help to make the change successful. Therefore, Change Leaders, facing challenging and continual change, will need to develop their capability to build and maintain relationships.

One tool that a leader must use is holding change meetings to discuss implementing the change. The more change, and the more that you need commitment from your team, the more you will need to conduct change meetings. Even if it is difficult, and team members have a hard time getting together, change meetings are an essential tool for leading change.

As a manager you have always led meetings, and you may feel that you have this skill in abundance. In this workshop, we are suggesting that the type of meeting that you use to deal with a change, and the skills that you can use to make these meetings effective, are broader than you currently believe. One of the goals of this workshop is to enhance your ability to lead change meetings, and motivate you to use them more frequently.

After this workshop, we recommend that you return to your teams, even if they are somewhat dispersed, and have a series of meetings to discuss change.

Within the framework of a change meeting, the Change Leader will:

- Announce a change and explain the need to change

- Get people's feedback, reactions and responses to the change

- Move toward commitment of the team to the change

- Plan next steps and actions by the team to succeed at change

The key concern of a Change Leader, is "How do I get my people to want to change." Too often, leaders approach this by pushing, by forcing the issue or demanding that people change or else. Gaining commitment to change involves getting people to make an internal commitment to doing what is needed to make the change successful. This does not mean not being passionate, or having people like the change. It is more like understanding that they have to change, and taking up the task. Managers in the past have focused on motivation by the carrot and the stick—reward and punishment. They believe that they need to coerce or demand that people change.

Helping Your Team Move Through Denial

Denial is the most problematical and prevalent organizational response to change and the greatest obstacle to real organizational change. The Change Leader needs to help people realize the reasons for a change, why they have to change, and why there can be no turning back.

Denial calls for leaders to gently but firmly confront denial in the team members:

- Give people information about why they need to change

- Confront passive behavior as you see it

- Tell people that they do not have the choice not to change

The key to leadership through denial is: When people remain in denial, you need to actively, but supportively, confront issues. Don't tell them what to do, just confront the issue and ask them to respond:

> "I see that you haven't done anything about learning new skills in response to this change."

> "I wonder what you are considering or feeling about the change?"

ACTIVITY: *Communicating Case for Change*

The Change Leader is responsible for communicating with and updating people on change. Explain that building and communicating an intelligent, comprehensive, articulate and persuasive change announcement is a critical success factor for the Change Leader. Encourage them to take advantage of the opportunity to grab attention, influence people's perception, and justify the change effort.

Managers are rarely accused of overcommunicating! But, sometimes they fail to appreciate that two aspects of communication are needed—content and compassion. Content communicates the data and facts about the change. Compassion communicates the human side, the feelings aspects of change. These two aspects are equally important and every good change communication should balance content and compassion.

Ask participants to think about the change they are about to lead or are in the process of leading. They should prepare a presentation to their group (or a replay of their communication process, if it has already taken place, or an announcement of an upcoming new change or part of the change).

> ***Ask:***   What are the best practices to use in communicating the case for change? Look for behaviors that resulted in a balance between content and compassion, confidence, energy, congruence between explicit versus implicit messages, body language, inspiration and leadership.

Listen to Resistance

Since change upsets routine ways of doing things, people are likely to be confused and upset. Feelings will result. Everyone will struggle with change in their own way. Leaders need to know how to wake people up, address difficult, complex issues, and deal with the emotional outpouring as people go through resistance.

Resistance that is out in the open is easier to deal with. When resistance is out in the open, leaders can get people together to talk about the issues. Too often, though, resistance is implicit and expressed indirectly. Leaders should make every effort to surface the implicit resistance and get it out on the table.

At a change meeting, after you present information about a change and get people to recognize the reality of what you are saying, they overcome their denial and you will begin to hear their resistance.

It will be much louder and more negative than denial, which was silent. Remember also, that resistance often comes in "code." That is, people do not own up to it. They present resistance as objections to the plan, as questions, or as difficulties.

Resistance responds favorably to intensifying involvement and interaction from the leader. Sharing time and being more available is one way to facilitate and accelerate acceptance of the change.

Present key strategies for overcoming resistance:

- Provide all information freely

- Listen to people's concerns—don't fix them

- Listen to your own feelings

- Help people see they are not the victims

- Help people learn and take the first steps

- Support troubled employees

II. Culture Lens: A Roadmap of the Big Picture

Every organization develops customs and patterns over time. These patterns represent the culture. Some suggest that strong cultures are higher performing and more successful. The concept of the culture lens is that change may cause people to lose sight of the meaning and purpose of their work. When attachments to old patterns and ways are broken, people may become bewildered and confused. Without the purpose and meaning expressed by familiar symbols, people can experience anxiety, loss of motivation, and loss of productivity.

Describe the features of your company's culture. Does it help or inhibit change?

A Culture Leader should be able to :

- *Inspire People In the New Direction*
  —Help a group put change into a broader context
  —Create a vision of where they want to go

- *Navigate the Shift from the Old to the New Culture*
  —Let go of old ways
  —Understand the new ways and why they are important
  —Define values and ways of working they need to move toward a vision

One of the first tasks of the Change Leader is not to give your people a direction, but to help them learn about and discover the direction they need to go and why they need to go there.

External forces create the need for the organization to change, adapt, or transform itself. (*Why we need to change*)

The vision is where the whole organization wants to go. (*Where we need to change to*)

The current state is the reality that you need to change from.

Moving across from the current to the desired state (*How we will change*): The organization must initiate a series of change initiatives which must be integrated and consistent with the overall direction of change.

The Change Leaders must help lead people to change, and develop the organizational capability for continuing change.

The Change Leader must help the team to understand this big picture of change and fit their efforts into that framework.

ACTIVITY: *Defining Key External Forces of Change*

The first part of creating the "change roadmap" is to document and agree on the specific changes that are taking place around you. These are the reasons for you to change, and they offer you some direction for how you need to change. You need to not just understand these yourself, but to explore them with your team, so that they can understand fully why they have to change.

Ask people to reflect on the major changes that are taking place in the environment around your company, in areas such as competition, globalization, technology, regulation, work values, and customer needs. Ask them to think about the most important specific changes that are right now affecting your company, and most particularly their own work unit.

Then, offer specific changes that are most affecting your company, and the implications of the change for the organization. Ask how your company will respond to each of them?

Mission and Vision: Creating Your Team Future

A vision is a picture of the desired future, what the organization (or work unit) wants to become under the most ideal conditions. The vision includes your mission, a statement of your core purpose, why it is important, the key values that you hold, and your customers. Your vision is what it will look like when you get to your preferred future. A mission and vision is essential for an organization or a work group to navigate through change.

It does not have to be a specific plan or set of goals, because these may change, but just offer an overall guide to where the group is going. Looking at the key elements that your company has defined in its vision, consider how your team can help achieve the desired changes.

Creating Team Mission Statements

One way to clarify how your team will help move toward achieving the strategic intent is to create a team mission statement. Until you are clear about your core purpose, your mission, you cannot create a vision of what it will look like. In this activity, we will take a first step toward articulating your team mission in moving toward the strategic intent.

It is curious that so few teams are clear about their basic mission. You should consider your mission in relation to how your team will work together to achieve your company's strategic intent.

A mission statement has several key elements:

We are _____	(Current role)
Who provide _____	(Product or service)
For what reason _____	(Purpose—why we do what we do)
To who _____	(Customer)

Using this framework, design a draft of your team mission statement.

Overcoming Cultural Obstacles to Change

Behind every organizational change there must be a shift in mindsets, the ways that people feel things should be in the organization. These common patterns of expectation are the informal culture of the organization. Most visions will require some major changes in the culture. That is because the culture arises from behavior and values that led the organization to its past success. They are hard to let go of because they have brought success in the past.

Ask for an example of an element of your company's culture that they might have to change or let go of in order to achieve the different parts of their specific team vision? Make sure that they get specific. They should mention things like the tremendous focus on individual results, or the greater degree of independence, leading to lack of coordination of efforts throughout the company.

Some parts of the current organizational culture become obstacles to achieving success at their team vision, in that if the organization or team does not change its cultural mazeways, its everyday ways of doing things, it cannot achieve what it intends. These cultural obstacles are not stated in words, but they underlie the patterns and ways of doing things.

> ***Ask:*** What does my team need to change? What obstacles does it need to overcome to keep on track to the desired changes? How can we overcome and get beyond these key obstacles to change?

III. Structure Lens: Aligning Roles, Tasks, Decisions, and Responsibilities

Change alters the clarity and stability of roles and relationships, creating confusion and uncertainty. The critical task for leaders in the structure lens is to determine if the current structure is appropriate for the new requirements. Leaders need to work with individuals and teams to realign the goals, roles, tasks, and work processes to support the change.

Let's say an architect designs a building as an amphitheater and halfway through the design, the project is changed to an auditorium. Does the design still work? Do the goals, roles, processes, and resources stay the same?

Whatever specific change your team or organization is going through, there are some general structural changes that must take place. The Structure Leader must focus attention on the changes in the group structure that are taking place as a result of the proposed change. Often some of the elements of the structural changes are not immediately obvious or explicit. If the structure is not changed, the whole change effort may be endangered.

Leaders must fully understand the requirements of the change, the nature of the work environment, and available resources in order to determine the framework of roles and relationships the team needs to perform the work.

Suppose a team is changing from being managed by a manager to being self-managed. One aspect of this change is structural. The team might begin by defining the change task using these kinds of questions:

- What are we being asked to do?
- What are the goals? Scope?
- How will we be doing things differently?
- How will decisions be made?
- What are the new boundaries and links between our team and other groups?

Gaining clarity about these elements would prepare the team to design a team structure (i.e., roles and relationships), to accomplish the task of becoming self-managing.

Some of the tasks of a leader using the structure lens include:

- ***Redefining Team Tasks and Roles to Add Customer Value***

    What the group has to do and how it will achieve success. What changes in your current work process must you make to deliver the greatest value to your customers?

    Most changes tend to broaden roles and ask people to learn more complex and open-ended tasks.

- ***Shift How the Leader and Team Make Decisions***

    Define how the group is accountable for results and make decisions.

    Most changes tend to push responsibility for results and decision making downward, and require people to make more decisions on their own, with less guidance from supervisors and more accountability.

Pyramid to the Circle

Point out that there is a general direction to the structural changes taking place in the organization. Most changes lead one to structures and processes that move along a continuum from the pyramid to the circle organizational structure. You have heard about breaking down the hierarchy, flattening the organization, empowerment, or the shift to a process organization. Most people are quite familiar with the hierarchial form of organization. Recently, organizations have begun to operate using a new structural form: the network, flat, and the process style of organization.

Suggest that the pyramid is not bad, but that dealing with change demands a flat, responsive organization.

Mention that whatever shift their work group is experiencing, it will also entail some shifting from pyramid to circle structures and activities. Understanding the broad context of this organizational shift can help them plan and implement their own change.

ACTIVITY: *Providing Customer Value*

One of the major ways that companies are shifting from the pyramid to the circle model is by asking employees to look at what they do in terms of how they satisfy and add value to customers, not how they serve the hierarchy. This means that individual team members have to take more responsibility for responding to customers, take more initiative, and act flexibly. It also means that some activities will have to change in order to provide greater value.

Many changes have to do with how you provide value to your customers. While many groups interact with external customers, some internal support groups are primarily concerned with supporting internal customers.

A leader must focus attention on how the team satisfies its customers.

ACTIVITY: *Decision Options*

The Change Leader needs to develop a collaboration with his or her team to facilitate their work together to design a plan for how they need to respond to the change. In most changes, the team is told what is expected of them, but there is a great deal of work for the team to come to agreement about how to get the desired results. The effective Change Leader will work with the team to design a plan, not try to offer a plan to them.

As a team changes, team members will be expected to make more decisions. But it must be very clear to each team member what decisions can be made on one's own, which are made together as a team, and which are made by the leader or the leader's leader. Since all of this is changing, the team needs to be explicit about who can make what decisions.

IV. Stakeholder Lens: Working Across Organizational Boundaries

The process of creating change within an organization is built on the cooperation of people representing several different roles which have different responsibilities, tasks, and difficulties in assimilating change. The people in each role have a different relationship to change. Successful and deep change, however, comes about not from one group changing on its own, but from an interaction of each of these different groups. You need to recruit support and help from other groups.

A *stakeholder* is any person or group that has a significant stake in the design and or implementation of a task, project, or effort. Stakeholders include:

- People in authority, such as your boss or corporate staff

- Influencers in the organization who have a lot of credibility

- Cross-functional groups with whom you must collaborate

- Customers and suppliers

- People who can obstruct or withhold support

- People who control resources (time, money, people, materials)

Your Boss as Stakeholder

The first and probably most important stakeholder on your list is your own boss, who is often the Sponsor of the change.

For other types of changes that you and your team initiate or want to do, you will need to actually recruit the support of a Sponsor. Sponsors are critical in that they give you what you can't provide for yourself—support of other parts of the organization, added resources, and visible leadership.

In order to define your own role in change, it is important that you are clear about what is expected of you, and the various degrees of freedom, resources, and outcomes that you are allowed. Many people set off with unclear expectations and lack of agreement with their own sponsor, usually their boss.

> ***Ask:*** Do you know your mandate, your role, and responsibility in this change? What changes can you sanction? What are the gray areas?

Architects and builders save thousands of dollars in lost time and effort by using agreements and contracts to clarify roles, scope, and project responsibilities. When a project undergoes a change in scope, they amend the contract to reflect the change.

If you are defensive, afraid, and distrustful with your boss, it will be hard to be different with your team. In some situations, you can feel that you are in a Catch-22 situation:

you are expected to do something, or deliver results, but you feel you lack authority, resources, or something essential to making it happen.

Clarifying expectations and agreements about change with your boss gives you an opportunity to test assumptions, renegotiate your role, and focus on those things that are clearly within the scope of your responsibility.

Plan a conversation with your Sponsor or boss where you talk about what you want to accomplish to help your team change, and what kind of support you need from him or her. Write down what you want to say and what you need, and share it with a partner.

ACTIVITY: *Stakeholder Analysis*

Most organizational changes tend to break down boundaries between groups and involve collaboration and even integration of tasks that are divided among several different groups. Therefore, many other groups will be involved in any change in your group, and many more people than members of your group will be affected.

The goal of the Change Leader is to get all of your stakeholders on your team not only to agree with and support your group and its change, but to become active resources to help you achieve success. In order to achieve this, you must listen to your stakeholders, and understand their needs, goals, and concerns.

There are far more stakeholders than just your customers; they include everyone who you have to work with, and who your work will influence. Stakeholders vary widely in style and intent. Some agree with and support your approach, project, task, or effort. Some disagree, some go along, some sit on the fence, and some are adversarial, and may work to undermine your effort.

Depending on how they want to be involved, and how important they are, you want to do several things with your stakeholders:

- Keep them informed of what you are doing

- Get them to agree with and support your changes

- Have them help you to accomplish your changes

Knowing the objectives, concerns, and personalities of people you want to influence helps you develop strategies to gain their support and cooperation. You may under-estimate your ability to influence these stakeholders because you haven't thought about what you have to offer or trade in connection with what the stakeholder wants.

Once you have analyzed the possible benefits to the stakeholder in exchange for his or her cooperation, you are ready to put together a strategy. Your strategy will be influenced by how attractive your offerings are; how much the stakeholder needs what you have, your prior relationship with the stakeholder, and your willingness to take the risks.

Strategies for Including Stakeholders:

- Share all information about the change

- Listen to their needs and concerns

- Spend time with them learning about their work

- Surface and discuss their issues (political, loss of status)

- Involve them early and frequently in the process

- Include them on the Change Team as resources

- Make sure they get what they want or need

Give some thought to how your team members may react to the need to work with different stakeholders, and altered strategies for winning their favor. Shifts in their support network, changes in the power base, and different interests, are now sources of conflict and altered agendas. Consider how you will deal with their reactions and the steps you will take to minimize the negative effects of change.

V. Information Lens: Creating Measures of Success

The information lens is concerned with providing the kinds of information a team or group needs to make informed, intelligent decisions, take action, track progress, and measure results. Teams need tools to help them know when they must recalibrate their actions to meet their goals.

Through this lens the leader:

- Locates information to enhance the team's daily productivity

- Shares information, consults on adjustments, actions, and assessing outcomes

- Evaluates and measures progress with the team

Think of the information lens as being like the instrument panel of a ship. The instrument panel is a system of gauges that provide information on speed, fuel, temperature, distance traveled, and distance remaining to help the pilot make critical decisions about the voyage.

Teams need similar navigational information to help them gauge the effectiveness of their efforts in accomplishing a goal. Once senior management determines the destination, the team designs a process for achieving the goal, and establishes factors for monitoring their progress and measuring results toward reaching the destination.

Too much information can be overkill. We want our teams to be doing the work, not spending endless hours monitoring, collecting, and reporting performance data.

The task of the Information Leader is to collaborate in helping the team get the information they need to guide the change. Everybody needs to agree on what will be measured and how. If they cannot agree, they are not truly aligned about the nature of the change.

One value of a collaborative effort to create a process information system is the development of a common vocabulary, with common definitions of goals and processes for reaching the goal. When extended to include cross- and multi-functional teams, this effort minimizes the problems in hand-offs from one team to another and reduces the barriers between functional silos.

Developing an information navigational system might begin with a process map that charts the critical tasks and capabilities required to accomplish the goal. A next step might involve integrating the map with maps from cross-functional teams. This sets up an opportunity to validate understanding of the goals and work processes, may trigger an early warning about obstacles, and may identify experts, unknown resources, or needed resources along the critical path.

Team Feedback
Dashboard

Real Time Process Measures
_____
_____
_____

Outcome Measures
_____
_____
_____

Warning Systems
_____
_____
_____

Defining Information Needs

Ask: What are some of the kinds of information teams may find relevant?

—Marketing information

—Customer satisfaction information

—Customer service data—time spent per service call, number of service calls, frequency, response time

—Inventory

—Employee concerns and satisfaction

—Financial—revenues, costs of goods sold, capital assets, debt, profitability

—Processes measures—order fulfillment, new product development, staffing levels

—Operations, manufacturing, testing, marketing

—Scheduling and milestones

Every change process must have specific information about how change is progressing. There are several types of information:

- *Process information:* ongoing, immediate feedback on the degree you are on course

- *Outcomes:* key success factors that measure your success at change

- *Warning Signs:* warning that you have a problem or difficulty

Your team's instrument panel should contain each of these kinds of information.

What Criteria Should the Team Use to Assess the Usefulness of the Instrument Panel Design?

- The number of gauges on the dashboard

- The goal is aligned with company's strategic goal

- Cross-functional team issues have been considered

- Input has been sought from cross-functional teams

- A system is in place for sounding an early-warning alarm

Creating Your Team Information Instrument Panel

Ask each person to consider the change they are facing, and write down what sorts of information their team will need in order to know that they are progressing on the change.

Write down several key measures that would help assess the effectiveness of the change. Try to find measures that are readily and quickly available, so that people can receive ongoing feedback on how they are doing.

Start with the key measures you have already used or determined to assess your success at change. Arrange them so you can keep your team on course in its journey toward successful change.

Use these questions to help guide your thinking about the change situation:

- What is the team's change goal? Describe the work processes that must change to enable the team to achieve the new goal.

- Are there cross- or multi-functional contributors whose collaboration is required to achieve the change goal? At what points do these contributors impact the work process of your team?

- What performance factors should the team be measuring? Why? How should they track and monitor progress? How will you expand their thinking about factors to measure?

- What information, feedback and expertise will contribute to the analysis and informed decisions the team must make to be successful in achieving the change goal?

- What information, feedback and expertise must you obtain to help you analyze and make informed decisions prior to taking action to implement your change goal?

Sketch a dashboard that reflects the factors and measures you will use to track and monitor progress toward your goal. What would you measure (schedule, milestones, cost, quality, satisfaction staff)?

Each person will make up a dashboard on a large sheet of flip chart paper, and share and post it.

Taking Your Instrument Panel Ideas to Your Team

The role of the Change Leader in the information lens is to gather information and present it to the team in a focused and useful way to help them move ahead. The dashboard you have created will be considered a first draft to take to the team as part of their change process.

Plan the process you will use to encourage and assist your team in developing a navigational dashboard of information to support them in modifying their work processes.

Next Steps: Planning with Your Team

At the end of the two-day Change Leadership Workshop, participants will go through a process to focus on how they are going to make sense of what they have learned and decide what to use and when. The choices are difficult, and you need a model to design and organize the different skills.

Think of the different change leadership skills as forming a menu. A menu places the different possibilities according to where they might best fit in the meal. In the same way, we can imagine that the skills of change leadership could be more or less useful at different phases of implementing a change.

When you return to your team, you will have the opportunity to communicate what you have learned, and engage people in what we call a "change conversation." This takes the form of holding a meeting to discuss some aspect of creating change.

ACTIVITY 2: Coach and Support Managers to Take Up New Roles

Develop the project management skills of the leaders of the new organization. Many of the new key players in the organization will quickly be overwhelmed with the task of implementing the change. The Change Navigator needs to make this process as easy as possible by providing tools and imparting skills in basic project management, including meeting management skills, planning skills and project tracking skills.

In order to support these changes, new leaders need several types of reinforcement:

- **Coaches** need to be available to support and help leaders develop and utilize their skills. Each new leader should have a coach who is familiar with the new leadership skills, and can help that leader assess and develop skills. It is not enough simply to train leaders, they need help and coaching to use the skills with their teams.

- **Leaders** need to assess their level of skills and define their developmental needs. Each leader needs assessment, learning, support and evaluation in their roles. It is not enough to just ask people to take on the roles; they need help to learn them.

- **Leaders** need to have their performance reviewed and their success rewarded according to the new skills. The coach is key to this process. The Change Leader must support and sometimes push their managers to learn their new roles.

Various guidelines for developing new teams are detailed in Task 3.

TASK 3: DEVELOP NEW TEAMS

Key Activities

■ *Redesign Teams*

■ *Develop New Team Charters*

■ *Develop Team Learning Process*

SETTING THE COURSE

The core of the changed workplace is a setting where people work together in new, more collaborative, more informed and more responsible ways. Work relationships have been shifted so that every employee thinks, feels and acts differently. This cannot be legislated, because people do not change by being told, they need to learn new ways, practice them, and be rewarded by success. Just as the leader needs to shift roles and let go, so employees need to take up different roles.

The change process has offered every employee options for new behavior and a new way of being involved. In this task, people cement and practice their new relationships in working together.

The new leaders pass on their new skills and attitudes to the rest of the team, and the Change Navigators support and coach them to be successful at this change. Together, teams implement the changes and assess their outcomes and results.

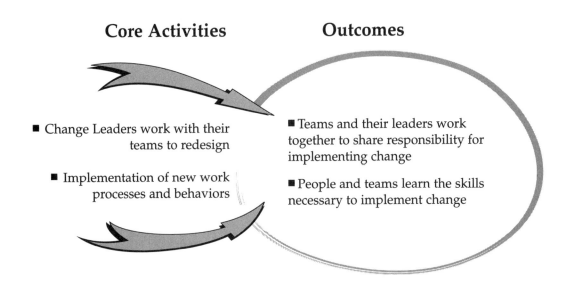

Core Activities

- Change Leaders work with their teams to redesign

- Implementation of new work processes and behaviors

Outcomes

- Teams and their leaders work together to share responsibility for implementing change

- People and teams learn the skills necessary to implement change

CHALLENGES

The New Behavior of the Leader Must be Matched by New Behavior from the Whole Team

If the leader changes, the team must be aware of the changes and take up a new role. Each team must undertake a conscious role and behavior shift. Leaders find it difficult to change unless they can be assured that the team members will take up new responsibilities.

Change is Affected by the Mindsets and Internal Assumptions of All Members of a Team About What Is Expected of Them

The new work contract must be implemented as a reality in each individual team. Some teams may interpret the new role differently.

GUIDING PRINCIPLES

■ ***Help the team or work unit choose the appropriate internal structure— how the unit works together as a group.*** This choice concerns the style of the group, the degree of direct control or autonomy of the authority and decision structure, how closely or loosely the group works together on tasks, and to what degree they are a group or a set of individuals working for one person. The other choices concern the degree to which people in the group perform different functions or the same task.

■ ***Define key processes and tasks.*** Today, the shift is away from individual jobs, to teams being responsible for processes and outcomes, and either making some role differentiations or becoming more generalists. The discussion of jobs should present this shift more clearly. Also, there is the issue of who should decide: the designer outside the team, or the team itself?

Every work group must decide to what degree work is being done by individuals, and to what degree it is being done collectively. This is the difference between working in a group or a team. A team is a coordinated set of people working together, and a group involves people doing similar work. Every group has to look at how much it is operating collectively and how much individually.

The account of individual work also needs to be in the context that fewer and fewer people in an organization can see only their own job, without looking at how it intersects with others, and how it is part of a greater whole system. The death of the individual job is happening fast. Also, satisfying customers puts more premium on individuals making decisions and on working cross-functionally and across boundaries.

KEY ACTIVITIES FOR TASK 3

ACTIVITY 1: Redesign Teams

Each team initiated a process of redesign, with the Team Leader and the rest of the team negotiating together how they will change. This is both a process of learning new skills and a collaborative design process in which each team decides how to accomplish the tasks and responsibilities they have been assigned in the new organization.

The Team Leader, who has gone through the Change Leadership workshop, has learned about a series of tools and team activities that he or she can bring to the team. The Team Leader, with the support of a coach or other facilitator if necessary, will be leading the team through a process of redesign. Each team will initiate a series of intensive team redesign meetings to implement change on a team level.

Determine How the Design Would Work

Making decisions about how to design a work group or team involves looking at the function of the work group and how the structure facilitates the task of the group. The design will be based on the function. When deciding on the elements of the design there are some critical areas to consider: What are the ways decisions will be made in the group? How will the group need to relate to other groups? and Where will the boundaries be between the processes? To clarify these questions, consider:

- **Roles**
  What do people do?
  How will they be held responsible?
  How is performance measured?
  How is success rewarded?
  What competencies do they need to get the job done?
  Do people do the same or different things in the group?
  How do people know what is effective? What measures are used?

- **Leadership**

  Who is the leader?

  How does the leader operate?

  What is the required style of leadership for the group?

  What is the level of authority of the group? The leader?

- **Decision making**

  How are decisions made?

  Who is responsible for what type of decisions?

  How much do individuals decide?

  —How much does the group decide?

  —How much does the leader, or external groups, decide?

  Where do decisions need to be made?

- **Boundaries/Interface with Other Groups**

  How do they relate to their customers?

  What are the inputs and outputs?

  What does the group do to create value?

  What support groups enable the group to do its work?

  How are they part of the group or work with the group?

  How is this group's work linked to other groups?

  How is information and knowledge transferred?

ACTIVITY 2: Develop New Team Charters

In order to clarify and learn a new way of working together, each team will create a new charter, clarifying how it will work and what it will accomplish.

Building on the results of their new understanding of their role and responsibility, each team, working with its leader, and sometimes with the aid of the team coach to facilitate the process, the team will create its charter.

The charter covers several areas:

Define the Mission (Purpose), Values and Vision of High Performance. The purpose or mission statement says what the group will do, and why it is important. This is usually a sentence or two saying we as a team do what, for who (what customers), to achieve what result. Usually a team feels that they know this, but when they actually clarify their mission they may find it more difficult or less clear than they expect.

The team must also talk about its values, how it will do what it does. This includes how people will treat each other, what will be assumed in meetings and in working together, and something about how things will be done.

Finally, the vision is a picture of how the team will look when it achieves the highest level of performance at its new tasks and responsibilities. This is an opportunity of the team to dream about what it could be doing, and explore new ideas. It is a very exciting process.

Articulate the Most Effective Style of Leadership. What is the most effective type and style of authority of the leader?

One aspect of this shift is that the leader is changing his or her role. No longer is the leader in control of the group, and the group a collection of followers. That role was one where the leader was directive, telling people what to do, and the group members were passive employees who did as they were told.

Today, more and more leaders are having to learn to let go of this traditional role and take up a more facilitative role. This role is one where the leader is a collaborator with the rest of the work team. While the leader in any group still retains some areas where he or she must make decisions and take responsibility, in more and more areas, as span of control grows greater, and the need for individual decisions grows, the leader will want to either share decisions with the team, get their input or delegate them to individuals.

This shift needs to be negotiated over time by the individual leader. It cannot simply be legislated or compelled in people.

Each team must decide how they will modify responsibilities—what each person can do on their own and what will be done by the leader.

The outcome is a new role and responsibility part of the team charter, which outlines how leader and team members will behave and what they can expect from each other.

Define the Process for Making Decisions as a Group. The task of the group or team and the leader is to create clarity about who makes each type of decision. A decision can be made for a group, by the group leader, by the group leader with input from others, by the whole group together, or delegated to individuals within the group.

Every group or team has issues that are decided by each of these levels of authority. In times of change and redesign, one of the most frequent changes is to shift decision making. Decision power today, in the new organizational models, often shifts down. People at lower and lower levels, as a group or individually, have to make more and more decisions. Every team and decision maker will find himself or herself passing decisions down or delegating more decisions.

It is important for the group to be clear at what level each type of decision is being made. Often different assumptions are made by different people in a group.

The matrix (page 203) gives you a format for clarifying the types of decisions that are made on each of these levels for your group or team. You should assess at what level the decision is made now, and looking to the improvements and changes that are anticipated, which group or level is the most appropriate level for that type of decision to be made.

ACTIVITY 3: Develop Team Learning Processes

Organizations, teams and individuals need clear information to see how their new actions affect the organization. In order to learn, change projects must provide the information a team or group needs to make informed, intelligent decisions, take action, track progress and measure results. Teams need tools to help them know when they must recalibrate their actions to meet their goals.

Each team should create a large, clear instrument panel, clarifying the information it receives on the most essential part of its operations and processes. The information should not just contain outcomes (output, costs, production, service calls, sales) but also measures of how the group works and how effective their processes are (percent of closed sales, number of mistakes or complaints, level of customer satisfaction).

Every change process must have specific information about how change is progressing. Developing an information navigation system might begin with a process map that charts the critical tasks and capabilities required to accomplish the goal. A next step might involve integrating the map with maps from cross-functional teams. This sets up an opportunity to validate understanding of the goals and work processes, may trigger an early warning about obstacles, and may identify experts, unknown resources, or needed resources along the critical path.

It is imperative to anchor organizational learning as detailed in Task 4.

TASK 4: ANCHOR ORGANIZATIONAL LEARNING

Key Activities:

■ *Convene a Learning Council*

■ *Define Strategies to Support Learning Throughout the Organization*

■ *Teach Skills of Learning How to Learn*

SETTING THE COURSE

Business philosopher Peter Drucker has said that the ability to learn is the only sustainable competitive advantage of an organization. No matter what you change, the future will contain further changes that will demand that the organization continue to change. Change has no end, even though everyone in the organization would like this not to be true.

The real intention of all these change processes is not to make one change. Rather, it is to develop capability across all levels of the organization to continue to change.

The means developing processes for capturing what has been learned in this change, and using this knowledge for future changes. The activities here should be implemented from the start of the change process and throughout it, not only at the end. They must be monitored and assessed throughout the whole change cycle. This final phase should be implemented through every phase of change.

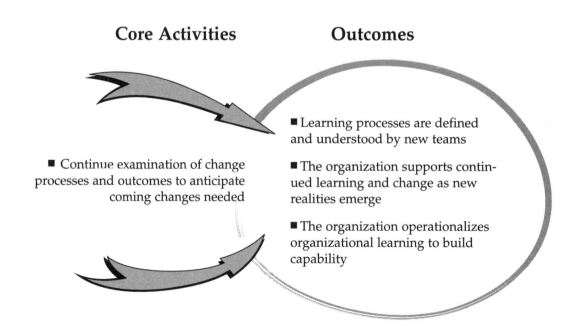

Core Activities

- Continue examination of change processes and outcomes to anticipate coming changes needed

Outcomes

- Learning processes are defined and understood by new teams

- The organization supports continued learning and change as new realities emerge

- The organization operationalizes organizational learning to build capability

CHALLENGES

Change Tends to be Reversible

After a change is implemented, people begin to forget the urgency, the need, and the wider purpose behind the change, and the organization begins to shift back to the old ways or loses its purpose and some of the intended effects. This drift back needs to be anticipated and the organization needs to design activities to prevent it.

Need to Internalize New Ways in the Culture

Organizational cultures, values, and systems tend to reinforce the old ways of acting, rather than the new ones. Changing at this level is one of the keys to sustaining change. The various organizational systems and structures have been realigned to fit the new workplace expectations and demands.

People tend to think they have completed the change when they act in new ways, and they don't internalize the implications of moving toward a new organizational form and style that need to be assimilated.

Organizations can change some things, but they may not learn the lessons of change and practice them in the next change process. If you make a change, but cannot make another change when you need to, then you have not really changed.

Overcoming the Drift to Closed Boundaries and Limited Information

An individual team, or an individual Change Leader may learn many useful new skills and attain change wisdom. If that person leaves and has not taught that wisdom to others, then the learning is lost to the organization. When people are tired or under pressure, they tend to keep their learning to themselves.

As teams implement change they also tend to keep to themselves, even if they have many cross-boundary activities. They especially tend to keep knowledge to themselves, and find it difficult to share with others. The organization needs to counteract these tendencies in order to have the capability of continual learning.

GUIDING PRINCIPLES

- **Develop organizational processes to maintain awareness of the change and encourage learning.** Changes tend to be undone by the culture, and there will be unintended consequences of any change. Every work group needs to look at what is happening in the change they are experiencing to keep on course. People must change but also learn the skills that make them capable of initiating and managing change in their group. Sustaining change involves a process of shared reflection on change and team learning. Learning activities must be supported, coordinated through the organization, and continually shared and acted upon. Organizational processes must support rather than conflict with these goals.

- **Take time out to evaluate whether the change process is achieving the forecasted benefits.** It is easy to lose sight of the overall goals and rationale for the process as each individual part takes on a life of its own. It is important for the consultant to continuously help the various levels of the organization to review the success and progress of the initiative and to plan ways of improving performance against the goals.

- **Do not focus on gaining short-term results at the expense of delivering long-term benefits to the client.** It is very easy to become sidetracked into delivering one part of the overall process and to miss the point that it was designed to achieve, namely the effective implementation of the change initiative. It is important not to lose sight of the overall goals and to build this into the assessment criteria of the sub-goals, tasks, and projects along the way.

- **Build a capability for organizational learning into the implementation.** It is not enough to change once; the organization must continue to change. This takes time, resources, and conscious intention. This includes finding ways to leverage learning from one part of the organization through the organization, codifying and expanding what is learned as part of the change process, and creating opportunities for many parts of the organization and many individuals, to continue their learning.

KEY ACTIVITIES FOR TASK 4

ACTIVITY 1: Convene a Learning Council

Early in the change process, as early as Wave One, convene a Learning Council, consisting of people from across the organization, to generate the lessons learned from change, and apply them to organizational development. This team of 2–4 people is responsible for creating processes at each phase of the change cycle to pull out the best ideas and processes, and recycle them into the organization.

These people should be trained in systems thinking, dialogue and other learning organization technologies. They should be part of each of the major activities of the change cycle as learning and capability development resources.

Gather teams together to conduct reflection sessions on each phase of the change process, drawing on the experience of the Change Team, various Change Leaders and stakeholders, to answer:

- What do we still need to do?

- Did we get the results we expected?

- Recall, record and share the history of the change.

- What can we learn from our change experience?

After each key change, the group should distribute information (using many media, including videotape) on what they have learned from the change that is useful to the rest of the organization.

ACTIVITY 2: Define Strategies to Support Learning Throughout the Organization

Build learning processes into each team. At regular intervals, stop the action and take time to capture the learning. This is kind of a status check on best practices; what we want to save. Reflecting on what we have learned should be conducted at the end of every element of the engagement.

Initiate internal conferences and multi-company activities to share learning. Bring together groups that have implemented major changes to share what they have learned, and draw out implications and lessons for the whole organization.

Hold large workshops to bring different parts of the organization together to share learning and best practices.

ACTIVITY 3: Teach Skills of Learning How to Learn

Define the skills needed for change capability and teach them throughout the change cycle. Define the skills related to capability that can be developed at each phase of the change process, and how they will be taught.

Learning skills include:

- Facilitation
- Visioning
- Project management
- Internal consulting
- Building high commitment participation
- Change planning
- Leadership and management role changes

Conclusion

The roadmap we have designed sets out an ambitious program for organizational change. Yet we see that nothing less than such total organizational commitment and engagement is necessary to achieve real, sustainable change.

The changes that organizations desire today cannot come about unless there is a fundamental change in the way people are involved as partners in the organization. Stepping up to these new roles and responsibilities demands a vast educational and redesign process that involves extensive learning, in a coordinated way. Organizational change is a community-learning process that involves many successive steps and large- and small-group learning activities.

No matter what form of new workplace an organization desires, there are certain human foundations and human relationship values, that underlie these changes. If the changes are initiated without the human foundation, the changes will inevitably decay and drift back to the original state.

No roadmap can detail all the sights, events and experiences of the journey. Every organization will pursue change differently, emphasize different elements, and have its own inner and outer imperatives to respond to. We have set out this roadmap to guide organizational leaders and navigators in making sure that they complete their journey.

Stay in Touch

We look forward to hearing from our readers about their experiences with organizational change.

You can contact us for further information, or to share your change experiences, at:

Changeworks, Inc.
461 Second St., #232
San Francisco, CA 94107
Phone: 415-546-4488
Fax: 415-546-4490
E-mail: djaffe@cworksinc.com
            cscott@cworksinc.com

Change Management Books and Resources

Dennis Jaffe and Cynthia Scott have published more than 100 professional articles, designed learning programs, conducted research, regularly keynote management meetings and conferences. Their work is captured in the following books.

Crisp Publications has published several of their books, including:

Take This Work and Love It, 1997

Managing Change at Work, 1989

Managing Personal Change, 1989

Self-Renewal: High Performance in a High Stress World, 1994

Empowerment: A Practical Guide for Success, 1991

Organizational Vision, Values and Mission, 1993

Their other books include:

Rekindling Commitment: How to Revitalize Yourself, Your Work, and Your Organization, Jossey-Bass, 1994

Working with the Ones You Love, Conari Press, 1991

Working with Family Business, Jossey-Bass, 1995

About Changeworks

Drs. Jaffe and Scott are founders and principals of Changeworks, a San Francisco consulting firm, with a national reputation for thought leadership in change management and putting strategy into action. Changeworks has a broad range of clients from start-ups to the Fortune 500.

Strategic Change Consulting

We work with organizations to create and sustain large-scale change efforts, including assessment of organizational and individual capability, building awareness of the need for change, and dealing with the effects of change on individuals.

Participative Re-design

We help organizations harness commitment and high performance through the development of self-managing organizations. By creating implements in productivity, technological innovation, new product development, business process improvement and knowledge management strategies.

Learning Materials to Support Organizational Development and Change

- *Strategic Illustration Maps*

  Visual maps that show the whole change process. Created to enhance communication strategies—get people to see the "whole picture."

- *Learning Modules*
  - —Leading Change
  - —Change Mastery
  - —Aligning Team Values, Mission and Vision
  - —Rekinding Commitment
  - —Empowered Teamwork

- ***Conversation Guides***

  Provides a framework for managers to inititate and lead conversations with step-by-step kits. Helps managers discuss key issues:

  —Leading in new workplace
  —Retention
  —Values into action
  —Overcoming resistance to change

- ***Keynotes and Briefings***

  —Visionary Leadership: Creating Commitment Through Collaboration
  —Managing Change: Thriving in Turbulent Times
  —Women as Leaders: Getting In, Staying In, Making a Difference

About the Authors

Dennis Jaffe, Ph.D.

Dr. Jaffe is a founding principal of *Changeworks* and a professor at Saybrook Graduate School, where he directs the Organizational Systems Inquiry doctoral program. Dr. Jaffe is a nationally recognized leader in the field of organizational change. He consults with major consulting firms, major corporations and family businesses to develop methodologies, innovative human resource systems, strategic plans and culturally transforative approaches to achieving results.

Dr. Jaffe earned his Ph.D. in sociology, M.A. in management, and B.A. in philosophy, all from Yale University. His professional training is in organizational development, and he is also a licensed clinical psychologist.

Cynthia D. Scott, Ph.D. M.P.H.

Dr. Scott is a founding partner of *Changeworks* and a national authority on mobilizing organizational capability and building change hardy organizations. She had lead over 20 projects related to mergers, restructuring, and downsizings, which included change readiness assessments, executive team visioning and alignment, large-scale strategic planning, work-process redesign and implementation management. She is known for her work in large group participative design and rapid strategy creation. She is a frequent speaker at conferences and a published author of ten books, her most recent *Re-kindling Commitment,* was an Executive Book club main selection.

Dr. Scott earned a doctorate in Psychology from the Fielding Institute, a Master's Degree in Public Health Administration and Planning from the University of Michigan and a B.A. in Anthropology from the University of California, Berkeley. She is a licensed clinical psychologist.

Janet Schatzman

Janet is head of the Strategic Illustration Enterprise at *Changeworks*. She has a national reputation in catalyzing the visual element of organizational communications. For over 20 years she has evoked images that transmit the meaning of complex organizational changes.

Her work has been applied to career management, visioning and values, process mapping, leadership development and team building. Her clients include Fortune 500 companies, government and community organizations. She has graphically recorded for such notable speakers as Faith Popcorn, Margaret Wheatley, and Mikhail Gorbachov.

Janet earned a Bachelor of Science Degree in Art Education from the University of Dayton and post-graduate work in Special Education with an emphasis on Art Therapy at Wright State University.

NOTES

NOTES

NOTES